Reviewing
Scientific Works
in Psychology

Reviewing Scientific Works in Psychology

Edited by

Robert J. Sternberg

American Psychological Association

Washington, DC

Published by
American Psychological Association
750 First Street, NE
Washington, DC 20002
www.apa.org

To order
APA Order Department
P.O. Box 92984
Washington, DC 20090-2984
Tel: (800) 374-2721
Direct: (202) 336-5510
Fax: (202) 336-5502
TDD/TTY: (202) 336-6123
Online: www.apa.org/books/
E-mail: order@apa.org

In the U.K., Europe, Africa, and the Middle East, copies may be ordered from
American Psychological Association
3 Henrietta Street
Covent Garden, London
WC2E 8LU England

Typeset in Palatino by World Composition Services, Inc., Sterling, VA

Printer: Automated Graphic Systems, White Plains, MD
Cover Designer: Michael Hentges Design, Alexandria, VA
Technical/Production Editors: Peggy M. Rote and Harriet Kaplan

The opinions and statements published are the responsibility of the authors, and such opinions and statements do not necessarily represent the policies of the American Psychological Association.

Library of Congress Cataloging-in-Publication Data

Reviewing scientific works in psychology / Robert J. Sternberg, editor.—1st ed.
    p. cm.
  Includes bibliographical references and index.
  ISBN 1-59147-281-4
  1. Psychological literature—Evaluation.   2. Peer review in psychology.
 3. Psychology—Authorship.   I. Sternberg, Robert J.

  BF76.8.R48   2005
  150'.72—dc22

                                         2005004730

British Library Cataloguing-in-Publication Data
A CIP record is available from the British Library.

Printed in the United States of America
First Edition

Contents

Contributors

Judith Amsel, former Executive Editor, Lawrence Erlbaum Associates, Mahwah, NJ

David P. Costanza, The George Washington University, Washington, DC

Alice H. Eagly, Northwestern University, Evanston, IL

Julia Frank-McNeil, American Psychological Association, Washington, DC

Paul A. Gade, U.S. Army Research Institute, Alexandria, VA

Elena L. Grigorenko, Yale University, New Haven, CT

Jonathan D. Kaplan, Army Research Institute for the Behavioral and Social Sciences, Arlington, VA

Leonard Martin, University of Georgia, Athens

Henry L. Roediger III, Washington University, St. Louis, MO

Robert J. Sternberg, Yale University, New Haven, CT

Abraham Tesser, University of Georgia, Athens

Gary R. VandenBos, American Psychological Association, Washington, DC

Preface

The motivation for this book was the realization that although many academics and others are called on to do reviewing, very few of them have any formal training, or sometimes, informal training, in how to referee. We who write all know how disconcerting it is to get a review that is either mindless or worse, savage. But what has the field done to correct the circumstances that produce such reviews?

Many of us have put our best faith efforts into writing journal articles or grant proposals, only to receive mean-spirited reviews.[1] A few years ago, I received a disparaging review of an article I co-wrote and submitted to a journal that referred to the submitted article as sounding like it was written by a "charlatan attorney" and that referred to parts of the article as "absurd" and as "gibberish." It compared the argumentation to that in "freshman-level term papers" and recommended that the author, who is "seriously out of his or her element with this topic . . . refrain from venturing into areas that exceed his or her professional competence."

Other comments in the review were not dissimilar to these comments. Fortunately, this review was "confidential," although of course, this confidential review was seen by the editor, other reviewers, and who knows who else. There was a second review of the article as well, which was very favorable.

Whether reviewers in other fields do the same, I do not know; I have heard though that when it comes to reviewing, reviewers in no other field attack their own in quite the ruthless way psychology reviewers sometimes do. What I do know is that more than once in my career, I have been stunned by the savagery with which my own work, and the work of others, has been

---

[1]See R. J. Sternberg (2002), "On Civility in Reviewing," *APS Observer*, 15, 3–34, and R. J. Sternberg (2003), "To Be Civil," *The APA Monitor on Psychology*, 34(7), 5.

attacked, usually under the cloak of anonymity. I have been surprised that the reviewers wrote what they wrote and that the editors (or heads of granting panels) sent back the reviews in such form.

Many other issues also arise with regard to reviewing. For example, a poor review might be imprecise, generally being critical of an article but not stating the criticisms in a way in which the author can profit. Some reviews are unconstructive. They say what is wrong but do not say how it can be fixed. Other reviews are wholly negative. They do not even have one nice thing to say to recognize the work the author put into the article. But it also does not help for a reviewer to be overly generous, failing to point out flaws in an article. A review may be biased, reflecting the author's own take on the field, rather than accepting that people in the field take different positions and that each position should be respected.

Professors spend some amount of time teaching students in graduate school how to write articles, but they spend little or no time teaching them how to review articles (or books or grant proposals). Perhaps they like to think that reviewing is a skill that just comes naturally to people. Apparently, it does not. Perhaps explicit training *is* needed.

The goal of this book is to teach anyone who does reviewing the basic skills needed to be a competent reviewer. These skills include competence in evaluating psychological work and competence in communicating that evaluation. The chapters cover a wide variety of review types, ranging from reviewing articles to reviewing grant proposals to reviewing book proposals. This book is for anyone who needs to review and who wants to ensure that he or she writes the same kind of review he or she would hope to receive.

To my knowledge, this is the first book of its kind. I hope you will find it to be helpful, and ultimately, I hope it is not the last book of its kind. Reviewing is essential to all sciences. It is a shame we have not taken it more seriously. In this book, we do.

Reviewing
Scientific Works
in Psychology

1

Reviewing Empirical Submissions to Journals

Abraham Tesser and Leonard Martin

S ooner or later almost every professional psychologist gets a manuscript to review. As you know, many publications that appear in professional journals have, as a central part, empirical data. Given the importance and frequency of the need to review such manuscripts, it is more than a little surprising that many of us receive little if any formal training in this vital service to the field. What makes this state of affairs even more surprising is the importance of peer review for the progress of science. Science is a social activity. It depends on the checks and balances provided by fellow scientists with expertise in the area. Such expert review cannot guarantee the legitimacy of the raw data nor even can it assure the heuristic value of the paper. However, it does increase our confidence that the results are appropriately framed in the work that has come before, that the procedures allow for an adequate test or exploration of the constructs, that the data have been appropriately analyzed, and that the implications derived by the author or authors are plausible.[1] The goal

---

[1] Naturally, every reader is or should be a critical reviewer of the information they are consuming. Readers ought not simply rely on the expertise of others as reflected in the publication in a peer-reviewed journal.

of this chapter is to provide general guidance for the neophyte reviewer and perhaps to provide a useful hint or two for more experienced reviewers as they approach the task of commenting on the suitability of empirical submissions for publication.

When the Manuscript Arrives

So, you have been invited to review a paper for the *Journal of Empirical Psychology*. The editor knows that you exist, and he or she is interested in your opinion. Moreover, the professional fate of a colleague, perhaps even a famous colleague, is, in a real sense, in your hands. What do you do? There is no set sequence or approach to this question. People differ in their style. We describe one generic sequence. This sequence reflects our own habits and the habits described to us by several others. Over time, as you complete several reviews, you will develop an approach that is comfortable for you.

First, take a quick survey of the manuscript. Read the title and the abstract, scan the introduction, and check out the references. (If you are cited, it is time for a glass of wine.) Your inspection of the manuscript should give you a sense of whether you would be interested in the paper, whether you have the requisite expertise, and whether you have the time to work on it. With this information, you are in a position to make your first two decisions: Are you a person who might have something useful to say about this paper, and will you be able to review the manuscript in the allotted time? Keep in mind that your first reviews are likely to be very time consuming. Both of us recall taking days to complete a single review. Moreover, it will almost always take longer than you estimate. Take heart, however; there is a learning curve, and with practice you will become faster and more confident in your reactions to the papers you review. If you feel you can generate a quality review and do so on time, you need to tell the editor.[2] Professional ethics dictate that you make these

---

[2]Note that often there is some slack in this deadline, but use it only if absolutely necessary. Late reviews are awful. They negatively affect the author

decisions promptly. If you are not able to review the paper, then it is often useful to provide the editor with names of colleagues who might be suitable reviewers for it.

Gatekeeper Versus Generative Mind-Set for Reviewing

The mind-set with which you approach the review can be consequential. For illustration we describe two philosophical points of view. Perhaps the most common point of view might be termed reviewer as "critic" or "gatekeeper." Reviewers with this mind-set see their primary goal as one of keeping bad research out of good journals. The focus is on finding weaknesses in the manuscript.

Clearly, it is your job to detect and report on critical weaknesses, but an overemphasis on this focus is problematic. There is a large literature that documents a confirmation bias: People tend to find what they are looking for (e.g., Gilovich, 1993). So, if you are looking for problems, you will find them. The fact is that any single study or even a set of related studies has flaws. Even the classic studies in your own discipline, when read carefully, yield problems. Indeed, that is one of the features that make them so rich: They generate a host of follow-up work that addresses questions about the initial interpretation or that clarifies the conditions under which the original interpretation holds. The point here is that you will find difficulties within just about any manuscript, and if you are focusing on finding problems, you may miss the potential, perhaps larger, positive contributions that may be in the paper.

There is another mind-set that might be termed *generative.* With this focus the goal is to find the positive contributions of the paper; that is, what the reasons are for accepting the paper,

---

of the piece, who is as involved in the outcome as you have been when your articles have been under review. So, courtesy demands a timely response. And, although you may be anonymous to the author, you are not anonymous to the editor, and late reviews reflect negatively on you.

where and how it advances the field, and how it might be revised to make these contributions more obvious or accessible to other scientists. Obviously the authors, the editor, and the field value this kind of read. But just as an overemphasis on weaknesses is problematic, so too is an exclusive focus on the potential contributions of the paper.

Our conclusion at this point is not hard to see. An overemphasis on either the gatekeeper or the generative mind-set is not nearly as useful as an integration of the two. One might ask, for example, whether the strengths outweigh the weaknesses. Are there ways to restructure the paper or reanalyze the data that might eliminate some of the weaknesses while emphasizing some of the strengths? Would the addition of another study bring the paper to the level of a publishable contribution?

Experience Counts

We believe that younger reviewers are more likely to overemphasize the gatekeeper function compared with more experienced reviewers. There are several reasons for the novice's approach. New reviewers often feel that their status as competent, hard-nosed psychologists is being evaluated on the basis of their reviews. From a new reviewer's point of view, it is more difficult and chancy to defend an opinion that the implications of an empirical paper are interesting or generative in spite of some flaw than it is to defend a negative evaluation that can be justified on the basis of factual statistical and methodological canons. Indeed, we believe that there is a general asymmetry in the field: It is often seen as better to be too harsh than too lenient. When graduate students are trained to read the literature carefully, that training seems to focus on finding the nonobvious methodological or statistical gremlins in the paper rather than finding the nonobvious or hidden productive implications for research.

Ego Involvement

Experience is not the only determinant of which mind-set a reviewer is likely to adopt. Reviewers are often ego-involved in what they are reviewing. For example, you may have a personal relationship with the author who is a friend, a former mentor, or a rival. You may have a bias for or against publication because the author is associated with a particular social category (e.g., small college, race or sexual preference, or gender). If you feel that an unbiased review would be difficult, you should let the editor know and recuse yourself from the doing the review. However, if you decide to do the review, where the possibility of these kinds of bias exists you need to be particularly careful.

More problematic is the reviewer's ego involvement in the substance and conclusions of the paper. Indeed, reviewers are often chosen on the basis of having published in the area of the paper being reviewed. In that case, publication of the paper has implications not only for the author and the field in general but for the reviewer's own career and ego. What personal buttons may the manuscript push, and how might this play itself out in terms of the balance between a gatekeeper and generative mind-set? A manuscript that supports the thrust of your own published work is likely to foster a generative mind-set. You as a reviewer may be motivated, perhaps implicitly, to see the strengths rather than the flaws in such a paper. Conversely, a manuscript that challenges the thrust of your own work may foster a gatekeeper mind-set. You may tend to frame even minor flaws as critical.

Did You Get Left Out?

An interesting case arises when the manuscript does not mention your own relevant work. After all, you know that your own work is seminal to the area—you said it before this paper existed and you said it better! Perhaps your first reaction is negative and biases you toward a gatekeeper mind-set. However, in our experience the reactions to not being cited are quite complex. On the one hand, failing to cite your important work is a sign of poor scholarship and could count against publication. On the other hand, ego involvement pushes a reviewer toward recognizing the general importance of the area and could count toward recommending publication. Regardless of whether you recommend in favor of or against publication, the question of how you deal with the omission remains.

There is some pressure against suggesting a self-citation in your review. If you suggest that the work be cited, then you run the risk of being identified by the author in what otherwise would be a blind review. At the same time you also run the risk of losing a bit of credibility with the editor, who may now think of you as defensive and egocentric. In spite of these pressures, if you really believe that the paper will be materially improved by citing or elaborating on your work, then you have an ethical responsibility to point that out. Note that pointing out the importance of your own work is really a generative activity and may be quite helpful to the author. Keep in mind, however, that there are reams of research indicating that most of us tend to see our own work as more important than do others.

We have drawn a distinction between the gatekeeper mind-set and the generative mind-set. We have recommended a balance between these two mind-sets. However, because we believe that the gatekeeper mind-set is more common than the generative mind-set, we wish to emphasize and call particular attention to the necessity for the generative mind-set as well.

Getting Down to It

Once you have agreed to do the review, put aside some time during the day when you are at your best and read the paper. Many people make notes as they go along, and that seems like a good strategy. This first read should give you a general idea of the quality of the piece and the location of any specific problems, ambiguities, and so forth. For several reasons, you will want to come back to the flagged areas before drafting a set of written comments.

First, your understanding of the flagged material may change as a result of having read the entire manuscript. As the Gestalt psychologists have pointed out, specific elements often change their meaning when viewed as part of a whole. You may also want to return to grapple with a difficult conceptual point and come to some resolution. It may be that the authors' reasoning is flawed. Perhaps the authors are right but have not clearly expressed themselves. If it is simply a communication problem, then you are challenged to suggest to the authors a clearer way of framing the issue.

Another reason to go back over the paper, particularly the flagged areas, is that sometimes the authors' use of theoretically relevant words and phrases changes from one section of the paper to another. You may want to go back to the definitions presented early in the paper and compare them with the use of the constructs later in the paper. Finally, rethinking each of the flagged issues may lead you to a totally different view of the paper: Further analysis of what initially seemed like minor issues may turn out to be more serious ones. Or, your attempts at integration may sometimes lead to the insight that the paper is making a much more profound point than appeared initially.

What Are the Authors' Goals?

Studies At the Descriptive Level

Empirical manuscripts vary in terms of the authors' goals. The particular aspects of the paper that are crucial for evaluation differ by goal. At one level, the goal of the research may simply be description. For example, what is the distribution of "life satisfaction" as a function of wealth, education, and so forth among citizens of the United States? This kind of question does not test a specific theoretical position or orientation, nor does it test a specific hypothesis. What is at stake here is the detection and enumeration of existing patterns of characteristics and responses.

The evaluation of a paper with this goal puts its primary emphasis on the data. Are they reliable? Is the sample appropriate and representative of the population? Do the measures, even on the face of it, reflect what the authors are interested in and what they address in their submission? Because the assessment of causal impact of one variable on another is rarely at stake, the terms *dependent* and *independent variables* are not entirely appropriate. In recognition of this language difficulty, we use the term *variable of primary interest* when referring to the variable that is analogous to the dependent variable.

One of our favorite examples of descriptive research has been reported by Mihalyi Csikszentmihalyi (1990). Csikszentmihalyi was interested in the ecology of feelings. Under what conditions do people report positive feelings and under what conditions do they report negative feelings? His methodology was straightforward. He simply equipped each of his participants with a beeper that would signal the participant at random times. The participants' job was to note the social and physical circumstances that they found themselves in and their feelings at the time of the signal. Csikszentmihalyi then compiled the results and was able to make some inferences about the frequency of positive and negative feelings, the circumstances under which individuals are most likely to be happy (e.g., at work), or the circumstances under which individuals are likely to be unhappy (e.g., around their children).

In this study it is difficult to establish causality. We can, however, learn a lot about the frequency distribution of positive and negative feelings over circumstances and about the association of mood and circumstance. Confronted by a paper like this, the reviewer should be focusing on at least two technical questions. First, is the measure of feelings adequate? By this we refer to reliability and validity: Is the measure of feelings reliable enough to allow for meaningful differences between people or conditions to be detected? Does the mood measure reflect what the author is talking about in the manuscript? This is clearly a question of validity. (Most reviewers will have had technical training in the types and assessment of reliability and validity, and a detailed discussion of these issues is beyond the scope of this chapter.)

When the goal of the paper is descriptive, the type of validity most frequently assessed is face validity—does the measure look like it reflects what the author says he or she is measuring? For example, suppose the author is interested in the mood produced by a movie. Recording the participant's evaluation of the movie, whether he or she likes or dislikes it, need not reflect the mood that the movie produces. Although there is generally a positive relationship between mood and evaluation—we like things that make us feel good and we dislike things that make us feel bad—this is not always the case (e.g., Martin, Abend, Sedikides, & Green, 1997). Sometimes we can like a movie that makes us sad or angry. By the same token, knowing that a participant likes or loves his or her children does not necessarily mean that the presence of those children always produces a positive mood.

The second technical question parallels the first but focuses on the reliability and validity of the factors the author is trying to relate to the primary measure. In Csikszentmihalyi's case it was settings such as home (and room in home), work, leisure, people, and so forth. Do these categories make sense? If they are based on personal judgments, then are the judgments reliable? If they are aggregates, has the investigator aggregated variables that have some logical or empirical relationship to one another?

Developing and labeling variables requires some ingenuity on the part of the author. At least as much ingenuity is required of the reviewer. Take, for example, the category *leisure*: If a participant is at his or her place of work and surfing the Internet in pursuit of a hobby, should this be classified as work or leisure? A reasonable case can be made for each. However, the case should be made one way or the other by the author. Finding reliable differences among constructed categories presents a prima facie case for the reliability of the categorizations and the primary variable. It is important to remember that the primary variable or dependent variable is not the only variable that should be assessed in terms of reliability and validity. All of the variables, including the variables that influence or co-occur along with the primary variable, deserve this kind of scrutiny.

Finding differences between categories on the primary measure implies at least minimal adequacy of the primary measure and the categorizations, at least with respect to reliability. Even in descriptive studies, positive results are more informative than negative results. We would suggest that questions about reliability become particularly important when there are no reliable associations in the data. A lack of association could reflect at least two quite different things: The variables were operationalized so imprecisely that it was not possible to detect the association, or there is no association to detect. As a reviewer, you will have to make some judgment about this. A minimal follow-up in the case of a failure to find an association is to make sure that reliability information about all the variables is present in the report.

Another technical issue that must be addressed when reviewing a paper with a descriptive goal (and at every other goal level) is statistical adequacy. Most of us have had considerable training in statistics, and, unless the paper is particularly technical, we are at least minimally competent in making judgments in this domain. Perhaps the most distinctive statistical concern with papers that have description as the goal is "fishing" and the error rate problem. When the goal is description, there is a tendency to measure everything that the author (and his or her students) thinks is relevant. That can be a lot of variables. The number of potential tests for associations among all these variables is very large indeed. For example, with 10 variables the potential number of tests is 45 $[(N \times (N - 1)/2)]$. Clearly then the reviewer, particularly under these circumstances, must be sensitive to the possibility that significant associations might simply reflect Type I errors. Of course, descriptive studies are not the only context in which this is a problem, but it does tend to crop up frequently in this context.

Technical issues such as measurement and statistical adequacy are important but not nearly as important as the substantive contribution the paper makes. A paper that has serious technical flaws leaves a reader knowing very little about the potential story that the data could tell. Such a paper should not be published. This does not mean that a paper with minor or no technical problems is necessarily publishable. There are other concerns as well.

Science is a social activity. The reason we publish papers is to disseminate our findings among other researchers. Therefore, a paper must communicate. A good paper is clearly written, and it is appropriately framed. If you as a reviewer are confused about what the author is saying, then it is almost certainly the case that others will be confused. Your job is to locate those ambiguities and, if possible, make suggestions regarding their clarification. Lack of clarity in itself is not a reason for rejecting a paper. It is a reason to ask the authors to clarify and resubmit. If a paper is too difficult to understand, you may not be able to give it a substantive review; you should then advise the editor of this. The editor can decide whether to seek another reviewer, to ask for a clarified revision, or to reject the paper.

Even a clearly written paper should be framed appropriately. You as reviewer, as an expert in the area of the paper, have a responsibility to make sure that the authors are aware of the relevant literature and the implications of that literature for their work. Are there landmark papers that have been ignored? Are there results from a related literature that bolster or contradict the present findings or conclusions? Has the author discussed the implications of his or her own results for the literature in general? If the answers to some of these questions are no, then a helpful review would point the author in the appropriate direction.

The most important criterion for judging a paper turns on the substantive contribution the paper makes. This contribution is judged by the reviewer's answers to the following questions. Is there anything in the paper you did not know before? Is there anything that is surprising in the results? Do the results qualify or reverse common knowledge? Will they stimulate further research? Csikszentmihalyi's work discussed earlier provided a positive answer to each of these questions. For example, Csikszentmihalyi noticed that some people were actually happier at work than at leisure. This observation was not anticipated by common knowledge, nor was it anticipated by the then extant theories of motivation. So, it was clearly informative. It contributed to a stream of research by Csikszentmihalyi and others on what has come to be known as *flow* (Csikszentmihalyi, 1990); it also helped us realize that our common knowledge or lay theories of the causes of mood are often wrong. Of course, there is no way to know for certain whether a paper will turn out to have an important impact on the field. However, by considering your own answers to the questions posed in this paragraph, you will have an informed, even if fallible, gauge on which to base this crucial judgment.

We are arguing for the value of surprising and counterintuitive conclusions. Papers containing such conclusions, however, may warrant extra scrutiny. Some have suggested the necessity of supporting extraordinary claims with extraordinary proof. Thus, if the paper is attempting to make a particularly counterintuitive point, then greater stringency is necessary when evaluating the technical aspects of the paper. We see this suggestion as a double-edged sword. On the one hand, prior knowledge of a phenomenon should affect your level of skepticism, as suggested by the "extraordinary proof" viewpoint and by Bayes's theorem. On the other hand, this increased skepticism could lead to a bias against accepting papers that challenge existing knowledge and open up new frontiers for understanding. You, as a reviewer, will have to weigh both of these consequences in making your recommendations.

Usually the first foray into a new research area is the descriptive study. As noted, the goal of such studies is to describe the landscape: how many widgets are out there, where you are likely to find more or fewer widgets, and so forth. The reports will consist of frequencies and covariances. In the best of these, the author will try to characterize the data in meaningful ways rather than simply presenting a laundry list of findings. The concerns that the reviewer must bring to bear at the descriptive level are also required at the next level, along with some new concerns. What is new at this next level is the author's concern with testing ad hoc hypotheses.

Studies That Test Ad Hoc Hypotheses

A specific hypothesis is an a priori expectation of a particular outcome. An investigator may hypothesize, for example, that rich people tend to be more satisfied with life than do poor people. The hypothesis may be one of simple association, but more often than not there is the implication of causality. For example, whether explicitly stated or not, the author may be implying that the possession of money or resources produces happiness. We use the term *ad hoc* to distinguish hypotheses at this level from hypotheses that may be derived from a formal theory.[3]

The major new concern in reviewing papers with ad hoc hypotheses is the plausibility of the causal inferences often made

---

[3] This distinction is not one that is hard and fast. One person's theoretical derivation may seem to be an ad hoc expectation from another's point of view. Whether the hypothesis is ad hoc or theoretically driven is consequential for the reviewer. Theoretically driven hypotheses add a layer of reviewing complexity that is absent in papers with ad hoc hypotheses. We discuss this complexity later.

or implied in this context. This is where your training in basic methods will come in handy. Even your first course made clear the distinction between correlation and causality. As we all know, a correlation is ambiguous because it does not distinguish among the following causal scenarios: A causes B, B causes A, or C causes A and B. We do not dwell on the statistical aspects or design issues such as random assignment or temporal order of this important issue. Doing so would take us too far afield, and almost all graduate programs train people to understand the advantages of random assignment and the special correlational tools and designs that are useful for untangling questions of causality. We do, however, spend a bit of time talking about confounding and other, perhaps more subtle, issues that arise in this context.

Confounds. Where specific hypotheses are at stake, the question of alternative explanations of a relationship between the independent and the dependent variables is central. Alternative explanations are accounts of the relationship detected by the author that plausibly differ from the interpretation offered by the author. The following is a fictitious example.

To test the hypothesis that social friction is bad for physical health, Smith introduced a Garrulousness Scale (the tendency to be argumentative in social relations). He found that participants high on garrulousness were likely to complain more frequently about headaches than were participants low on the scale. Smith concluded that argumentative relationships have negative consequences for one's health.

It is possible that Smith is absolutely correct; the data do show a relationship between the individual difference measure of interpersonal strife and headaches. However, there are also a number of alternative explanations for this result. For example, neuroticism, an individual difference construct that has been used frequently in the psychological literature, provides one such interpretation. Because neuroticism is associated with negativity in general, it could be associated with difficult interpersonal relationships. Neuroticism is also associated with complaints of physical symptoms. The Garrulousness Scale may be, at least in part, a reflection of neuroticism. An alternative explanation of

Smith's data is that it is neuroticism, not necessarily garrulousness, that accounts for the relationship between interpersonal strife and ill health. The existence of an alternative explanation is a problem.

The most salient instances of confounding are cases in which a relationship has been detected. However, if a confounding variable has an opposite relationship with the independent and the dependent variables, then such a confound could obscure a positive association and may even produce a negative one between the two focal variables. Suppose, for example, garrulousness actually causes ill health. Suppose further that a third variable, hardiness, is positively related to garrulousness and negatively related to ill health. It would not be surprising in this instance that the empirical relationship between garrulousness and ill health is undetectable or in the wrong direction. If the confound hardiness were removed, then the hypothesized relationship between garrulousness and ill health would be revealed.

We should note at the outset that the problem for the reviewer (and the author) would be much easier to address if the study included good measures of the potential confound. If so, statistical procedures could be used to address the question. In the present example, partial correlations might provide clarification. When a measure of the potential confound is not available, however, the reviewer's judgment is critical.

Some questions for the reviewer are as follows: How serious is the problem, and what should you recommend? Should you suggest that Smith simply acknowledge the neuroticism interpretation? Should Smith drop the garrulousness interpretation in favor of the neuroticism interpretation? Or does the existence of a plausible neuroticism interpretation call for rejection of the paper? One way to determine the appropriate response is to consider the author's goal. If the author's purpose is simply description (i.e., reporting the correlates of his new Garrulousness Scale), then the neuroticism alternative is not a deal breaker. The evidence is that garrulousness is correlated with health, and that is true even if that relationship is based on their common connection to neuroticism. It is true even if there is a reverse causal arrow; that is, health affects scores on the Garrulousness

Scale. Although each of these alternatives might be true, they are beside the point that the study is attempting to document.

On the other hand, when the author is attempting to document a hypothesis, the causal interpretation is important. Under this circumstance, the alternative explanation can be damning. The existence of a plausible alternative casts doubt on the message intended by the author. As a reviewer, at the very least, you should suggest that the alternative neuroticism hypothesis be acknowledged. A more stringent recommendation would ask for more data in a revision or even a recommendation against publication.

At what level of recommendation will you weigh in? There are at least two sources of guidance. The first is the nature and status of the outlet. If the paper has been invited by the editor for an edited book or a special issue of a journal, then rejection or the recommendation to collect new data would be rare, and you would suggest that the authors discuss the confound or modulate their language to acknowledge the limitations of the data. The case of an unsolicited manuscript intended for a refereed journal expands the options. Here, the status of the journal makes a difference in your recommendation. The top-tier journals often require a more stringent evidential base than do second-tier journals. Your own experience and judgment will have to guide you as to whether the contribution is at the appropriate level for the status of the journal. The same manuscript is not equally acceptable to all journals. Indeed, as a reviewer, even if you feel that the paper is not up to the journal for which you are reviewing it, you can recommend a journal for which you think the paper would be more competitive.

A second source of guidance regarding your recommendations comes from the empirical context in which the confound is embedded. The confound may be central or related to a central aspect of the paper, or it may be incidental. The confound is more damaging if it is the central empirical outcome than if it is a secondary finding, and you should probably ask for additional data or reject the paper.

In a paper with multiple measures or studies, the confound may exist among several demonstrations of the hypothesized relationship. If the confound is restricted to one or a few cases, it is not as consequential as if it were common across demonstrations. Although there are advantages of triangulation (that we touch on later), multiple studies or measures do not necessarily erase the problem of confounds. For example, suppose Smith had multiple measures of interpersonal strife and multiple measures of physical symptoms that he had administered to several different samples. In spite of having multiple measures and samples, the confound remains in each instance. Neuroticism could be driving each of the replicated outcomes.

Testing specific ad hoc hypotheses adds several criteria that must be satisfied if the paper is to meet its goal. Not only must it satisfy the concerns mentioned in connection with descriptive studies, but it must also be evaluated in terms of the plausibility of causal inferences. Although a number of factors must be considered when evaluating causal claims (e.g., temporal order), we have emphasized the issue of confounding. We have done so because this common concern seems to create a particular demand for reviewer judgment.

Testing Theoretically Driven Hypotheses

At another level, the goal of the empirical paper may be to test a relatively general theory or model. This is distinct from testing ad hoc hypotheses in that the hypothesis itself is not ad hoc but, rather, derived from a particular theory or theoretical perspective. The derivation of the hypothesis adds another set of concerns that must be addressed by the reviewer. When testing a theoretically derived hypothesis or hypotheses, the authors will lay out a point of view that encompasses many more facets than can be dealt with empirically in the particular submission at hand. The author will use propositions from this perspective to derive a specific set of predictions. The derivation will be couched in relatively abstract terms, as will the derived hypotheses. As the paper develops, these theoretical variables will be translated into a set of operations.

For example, the theory of cognitive dissonance suggests that inconsistency between one's attitudes and one's behavior is uncomfortable and that the individual is motivated to reduce the discomfort by eliminating the inconsistency. Obviously, at this abstract level there is no way to test the theory. Therefore, the constructs are operationalized. For example, volunteering to undergo an arduous initiation into a group is inconsistent with the idea that the group is boring. So, according to the theory, an individual confronting a boring group will experience more dissonance if he has undergone a harsh, humiliating initiation into that group than if he has undergone a mild initiation. As a result of dissonance reduction, we would expect more positive attitudes toward the group with the harsh initiation than with the mild initiation.

Papers with theoretically derived hypotheses are demanding. In addition to the earlier considerations such as reliability, sampling, statistical adequacy, confounds, and so forth, the reviewer must also be concerned with the logic of the derivation of the particular hypotheses and the extent to which the operations reflect not only the common-language understanding of the variables, but also the meaning agreed on by researchers in the relevant research tradition.

Most psychological theories with which we are familiar are stated in abstract verbal terms. As such, these theories are open to interpretation not only with respect to the indicants of the crucial variables but also in terms of the underlying logic. A reviewer has the difficult job of making judgments on both dimensions: Do the operations actually map onto the theoretical constructs? What precisely does the theory predict? In theory-driven research, each section of the paper presents a different set of issues that must be addressed.

The Introduction. The introduction to the manuscript should give a comprehensive account of the theory and the derivation of the specific hypotheses to be tested. Is the presentation of the theory clear? Does it show sensitivity to previous research on the theory? Is the derivation of the hypotheses clear and compelled by the logic of the theory? The derived predictions need not conform to the reviewer's intuitive expectations but should conform to a clearly stated theoretical logic.

If, after having read the introduction, you are still wondering how the specific hypotheses were derived, there is a serious problem with the paper. In this case you should recommend that the authors clarify their logic. The introduction is also the place in which other theories that lay claim to the same domain should be addressed. Are competing theories presented clearly, or are they simply relegated to "straw man" status? (In this context, the *straw man fallacy* refers to presenting a distorted account of an alternative theory or position so that the alternative can be easily dismissed.)

The Method. The method section provides an opportunity to confront issues of operationalization, the translation of theoretical variables into concrete operations and measures. Note that as a reviewer you are often making judgments about an empirical paper even before looking at any of the data. With theory-driven research, these pre-data judgments are even more consequential. With theoretically driven measures, confounding remains a particularly important issue. Do the independent and dependent variables seem to reflect the appropriate theoretical constructs? When a variable is operationalized, that manipulation (or measure) is rarely pure: It sometimes falls short of everything implied by the construct, and it almost always has components that are irrelevant to the construct. Because of this, researchers often find it useful to use multiple operations or measures that vary in their detail but are all intended to reflect the same construct. This allows for *triangulation*.

Triangulation and Programmatic Research. When a manuscript contains several studies, you as a reviewer must evaluate the extent to which each of these studies meets basic minimal criteria for acceptability. With programmatic research this is not sufficient; attention to all the studies and their interrelationships with one another is crucial. Different manipulations of the independent variable, or different measures of the dependent variable, can provide converging evidence for generalizability and theoretical causal sequence. They do so because the different operations have the theoretical variable in common and the irrelevancies are all different from one another; that is, there is triangulation (Campbell & Stanley, 1963). Multiple studies with multiple operations are often a strength in theory-driven research.

However, the potential strength of multiple operations or measures can also be a weakness. A set of studies with different independent variables and different dependent variables may be little more than a hodge-podge. When confronted by a series of studies, the reviewer needs to think configurally. In judging the value of the collection of studies, the reviewer might address questions such as the following: Does one study answer questions or address ambiguities raised by another? Do they complement one another in tightening the case for the particular theoretical derivation at issue? In short, is the research programmatic? In doing programmatic research, often the investigator will stick with one operationalization of the dependent variable and will vary operations of the independent variable; or he or she might use a similar set of operations for the independent variable and vary the operations for measuring the dependent variable. If these multiple operations are to strengthen the case, then they should extend or clarify one another. Each of the studies may have a particular weakness, but they ought not to share this weakness. Thus, when considering the package of studies in programmatic research, the theoretical cause is a more plausible interpretation than is the weakness associated with any single study.

We have emphasized multiple operations and triangulation as a positive strategy for those conducting programmatic research because using the same operations makes the collection of studies more subject to plausible alternative explanations. There is, however, an argument that can be made for psychologists involved in programmatic research who use the same or similar operations in different contexts (Byrne, 1997). Reliability is easy to assess, the cumulative aspect over studies is clear, and the causes of different outcomes are highly visible.

We have focused on the theory-driven aspects of operations, and some of the concerns that reviewers might have about these issues. More generally, however, the method section is the place where the reader learns how the research was conducted. The reviewer also must consider the extent to which this section communicates precisely what was done and how the data were collected. A knowledgeable reader should be able to reproduce the research procedure from this description. Not all instruments need to be present in their entirety, but information about how or where they may be obtained should be there. New methods or measures should be more thoroughly described and justified; authors should describe their plans for assessing the adequacy and meaning of new methods and measures (i.e., manipulation checks). The part of the instructions that the author (or you as reviewer) thinks is crucial for the effects should be presented verbatim. As usual, there is a tension between the need for completeness and the pressure toward brevity. As a reviewer, you have to monitor that tension and make sure that crucial materials are included and adequately addressed but that extraneous and secondary details are deleted.

The Results. This section presents the statistical evidence that bears on the hypotheses. By this time, you know whether the investigators have manipulated and measured variables that are related to the theory. So now the question concerns the extent to which the data are consistent with the theoretical story. In a theory-driven paper, the reviewer should have a relatively concrete idea of what relationships are crucial and how the relationships should be manifest in the data before even looking at the data. Does the theoretical account anticipate main effects (simple correlations) or interactions (moderated correlations)? Is there a mediator? Was it assessed? If you do not have a concrete answer to each of these questions at this point, stop. Go back and reread the introduction. Either you missed something, or something crucial is missing from the paper. Authors frequently review theoretical expectations in the results section. This is often helpful, but do not let the author's review substitute for your own independent reading of what the theory predicts.

Now that you know what the theory predicts, you are in a good position to know what variables should enter into relationships and what the shape of those relationships should be. Did the author assess the relationships among the theoretically appropriate variables? Did the author assess relationships using appropriate statistical models? Is the author clear about the significance of each test for the theory? Is it clear which of the analyses are theory driven and which are exploratory? Are checks on the effectiveness of the manipulations reported?

Often results are roughly in the direction of the theoretical predictions. Sometimes authors will suggest that the fit is closer than might other people. As a reviewer, you will have to assess the extent to which this has gone too far. Some common clues include the following: The authors make tests of simple main effects rather than reporting the overall interaction when an interaction is expected, or a marginal effect is called significant when it confirms the authors' perspective and is called nonsignificant when it goes against the authors' perspective. Planned comparisons are legitimate and very powerful ways of assessing a specific hypothesis. However, such a comparison is difficult to justify if it does not flow directly from a clear understanding of the theory. Sometimes authors claim support from a nonsignificant pattern that emerged over more than one study or dependent variable. When the same pattern emerges in independent samples, one can assess the probability of that pattern using meta-analysis; when it comes from two, perhaps correlated, dependent variables from the same study, the assessment of its significance is dicier. This list can be extended almost indefinitely, but that is not the point. The point is that reviewers must have a firm fix on what the theoretical framework anticipates and what it does not. Evaluation of the results should flow from that.

Rarely are predictions confirmed or not. More usually it is a mixed case. Some predictions are on the money, some expected differences do not emerge, and there is usually a surprise finding or two. Given a mixed bag of results, what should a reviewer recommend about the paper? The recommendation depends on the mix. If the theory confirmations are simply a replication of previous findings in the domain, then the contribution is not as great as if the results confirm novel predictions. Results that appear to show new aspects while testing for and failing to replicate established aspects of a phenomenon are ambiguous. The findings leave unclear the relationship between the new results and the established results. If the predictions confirmed are the same predictions that flow from alternative formulations, then the contribution is not as great as if the results uniquely support a particular theoretical formulation. "Common wisdom" or common knowledge is often a predictor of outcomes too. Results that confirm the theory but also confirm common wisdom are less interesting, informative, and provocative than are results that seem to question the common wisdom.

The reviewer's recommendation need not be a direct function of the extent to which theoretical derivations are confirmed. Sometimes there is a surprise in the data that is so robust and so interesting that it demands publication. Even if the finding is not consistent with the theory, it may be sufficiently interesting that it will attract additional research and attempts at explanation.

Again, a reviewer must be concerned with the tension between completeness and brevity. A few means can be more succinctly reported in the narrative than in a separate table. Sometimes a picture (graph) is worth a thousand words, but when it is not, it need not appear. The detail of a statistical analysis can be difficult to follow. If this is the case, and if you can think of a simpler or clearer way of presenting the necessary detail, then the authors and the potential readers should welcome the suggestion.

The Discussion. The discussion section of a theory-driven empirical paper should summarize the theoretical issues at stake and provide an account of the implications of the data for these issues. Here a reader should learn in broad, abstract terms where the theory was supported and where it fell short. The author is expected to be accurate in this accounting and to either modify the theory to account for anomalous results or provide an explanation for the anomalies. You as a reviewer need to ask if the explanations are plausible and if the suggested changes in the theory are likely to be productive or counterproductive (i.e., if they undermine the major thrust of the theory). Moreover, if you have a suggestion to make, particularly in accounting for anomalous results, feel free to make it—the author might appreciate it! This is also the place where the author should relate his or her finding to other theories in the domain. Again, it is important that these alternatives are presented fairly and not simply as straw men. The theory being discussed may have a series of intervening steps between initiating conditions and outcomes. The research may have operations only reflecting the instigating conditions and the outcomes without any direct measure of the intervening steps. If the outcome conformed to prediction, then there is evidence that is consistent with the more complex theoretical apparatus, but this does not provide direct support for the intervening apparatus. Only the input and the outcome were observed. The author's language should reflect this distinction and not claim that the data directly support the intervening process.

Author claims about intervening processes should be closely examined when there is an alternative competing theoretical explanation that is also supported by the pattern of outcomes (i.e., when there are two theories that predict the same relationship between the independent and dependent variable but do so through different intervening processes). In this case, the results are consistent with the author's theory but do not favor it over the competing account. As a reviewer, you are also the defender of the voiceless: namely, the proponents of the competing perspective.

In the discussion section the author should review the findings and make extrapolations to other theoretical or applied domains. The discussion should not be a simple rehash of the results with little in the way of the broader implications of the results. Nor should the discussion be a series of speculations with little grounding in the specific outcomes of the reported research. Although the author is encouraged to discuss implications of the results for larger theoretical, social, and other applied issues, this license for extrapolation does not extend to the fit between theory and data. The reviewer should hold the author's feet to the flame with respect to the latter.

Some General Caveats

Common Misplaced Criticisms

Easy, but sometimes misplaced, criticisms for reviewers to make with regard to many empirical studies are as follows: All the participants are college students, or only male participants or only female participants were included. Or the study is artificial—it is done in the lab and in a very short time. Or the methods are artificial. Or only a single culture is represented. Often this kind of criticism is raised as if it explains or, more commonly, dismisses the results and the author's interpretation of the results. However, positive results (i.e., a relationship between the independent variable and the dependent variable) cannot be explained by a constant. If all the participants are college students, then neither the independent variable nor the dependent variable is correlated with school status. So, school status cannot explain the relationship and the criticism is logically wrong.

Although the kind of concerns alluded to above cannot explain (or dismiss) a set of relationships, they can be legitimate concerns. However, when they are legitimate they address the moderation or generalization of findings. And, they do not always do this successfully. When raising questions of limited generalizability, there must be a plausible story for why the results might change under different circumstances, methods, or participants. For example, Sears (1986) has persuasively argued that research with college students may not be generalizable to a number of other populations. College students are still forming their identities, so studies showing changes in self-construals may not be easily generalized. College students are generally brighter than nonstudents, so studies of problem solving may be limited in generalizability. Each of these distinguishing features may be relevant to a particular finding (e.g., issues of change in self), but they are not automatically so. If the reviewer is concerned about such issues, then he or she cannot simply stop with the observation that the only participants were college students. A plausible case must be made for that being a constraint on generalization.

Other Concerns

An Asymmetry Between Acceptance and Rejection. Reviews that ultimately recommend acceptance or rejection should on the average be shorter than reviews that recommend revise and resubmit. If you recommend rejection, you need only refer to the critical flaw or flaws of the paper. Pointing out every blemish is overkill. Your goal is not to educate the author nor is it to put the author in his or her place. If you recommend acceptance, then you should specify the basis on which you make that recommendation. You need not write a letter of commendation.

The revise-and-resubmit letter is probably the most common and most difficult to write. In this case you need to be quite specific about the things that need changing and provide recommendations for how they should be changed. If you recommend the collection of new data or new analyses, you should specify the outcomes that would warrant a more positive editorial response and the outcomes that might raise additional concerns. Even here, however, a comment on every aspect that occurs to you is unnecessary. Stick only to the features that you believe are central for making the ultimate decision regarding publication. Your recommendation and suggestions should be clear and concise.

Political Versus Scientific Merit of the Conclusion. Sometimes empirical data are related to issues surrounded by social controversy, for example, race differences, gender differences, or adequacy of gay parenting. The data may reveal differences that are easily interpretable in socially undesirable ways. As a reviewer, you should be aware that your review will be more closely scrutinized under these circumstances. Our general advice is that, as always, you should be as careful as you can possibly be and that the scientific merit of the work should drive your recommendation. Although it is unlikely that you would have to defend your recommendation, you should be prepared to do so. We also feel that a pragmatic comment is warranted. If the paper flaunts a conclusion that challenges conventional morality, then prudence suggests that the author not overgeneralize or abstract beyond the data. If the paper warrants publication on the basis of scientific merit, then as a reviewer you might suggest that the author stick to conclusions that are as close to the specific data as possible.

No Ad Hominem Statements—Respect for the Author. It should go without mention but regrettably it cannot: Reviews should always be about the work and not about the author or the reviewer. Regardless of your personal feeling about the intelligence, moral standing, family heritage, or looks of the author, you should do your best to keep these feelings from being expressed either directly or even indirectly. This caveat holds for positive feelings as well as negative feelings. When your review is drafted, go over it again just to make sure that personal references do not appear.

Feedback on Your Review— Did You Get It Right?

You completed your review perhaps months ago. You sent it to the editor and have almost forgotten about it when an envelope appears in your mailbox bearing the journal's logo. It contains the editor's disposition letter and the comments of the other reviewer or reviewers. Did you get it right?

Here are the clues you are most likely to check out. Was your overall recommendation the same as that of the other reviewers and the editors? Are the concerns you raised similar to the concerns expressed by the other reviewers and referred to as important in the editor's disposition letter? Do not be discouraged if you see something in the other reviews that you missed in your review and that in retrospect you think is crucial. This will happen. Sometimes it will happen to you and sometimes you will be the one to point out something the others missed. Reviewers are often chosen for their unique expertise. It is not surprising that there are differences in what things are picked up and how they are weighted. So, regardless of the ultimate disposition of the paper and what other reviewers said or did not say, if you gave the paper a timely, careful read and were fair to the author in your assessments, then you got it right.

References

Byrne, D. (1997). An overview (and underview) of research and theory within the attraction paradigm. *Journal of Social and Personal Relationships, 14*, 417–431.

Campbell, D., & Stanley, J. (1963). *Experimental and quasi-experimental designs for research.* Boston: Houghton Mifflin.

Csikszentmihalyi, M. (1990). *Flow: The psychology of optimal experience.* New York: Harper & Row.

Gilovich, T. (1993). *How we know what isn't so: The fallibility of human reason in everyday life.* New York: The Free Press.

Martin, L. L., Abend, T., Sedikides, C., & Green, J. D. (1997). How would it feel if . . . ? Mood as input to a role fulfillment evaluation process. *Journal of Personality and Social Psychology, 73,* 242–253.

Sears, D. O. (1986). College sophomores in the laboratory: Influences of a narrow data base on social psychology's view of human nature. *Journal of Personality and Social Psychology, 51,* 515–530.

2

Reviewing Articles for Methods

Robert J. Sternberg and Elena L. Grigorenko

F elix Floogleflitter concludes that humans and other animals are not the only ones with feelings. Plants have feelings too. How does he know? He grows a set of 100 plants in one room of a house. He creates a happy mood for these plants, piping in happy music to them, playing happy TV shows in the background, and every day giving them a positive inspirational message about his belief that they can grow to be big and tall. He places another set of 100 plants in a different room of the house. He creates a sad mood for these plants, piping in sad music, playing depressing TV shows in the background, and telling them every day that they are failures as members of the plant kingdom and that their growth will be stunted. After 2 months, he finds that the "happy" plants have indeed grown significantly more than the "unhappy" ones. He is mortified when a prestigious journal rejects an article of such monumental importance.

This obviously fictitious example points out the importance of methodological rigor in empirical studies. The study was blatantly flawed. Did Flooglefitter randomly assign plants to the two conditions? Were the rooms equivalent in their exposure to sunlight? Did he water the plants in the two rooms equally? Did he control for soil? Did he make sure room temperatures and humidity levels were the same? No matter how monumental a finding may seem to be, if it emerges from poorly designed research, it is worthless. One really can validly conclude nothing at all.

Let us start with how not to review for methods. The way not to review is to have a set of methods you prefer—experimental ones, biological ones, or whatever—and then judge what you read in terms of the extent to which it matches your preconception of how whatever problem is being studied really should have been studied. Bad reviewers require that studies follow a methodology that they, in their infinite wisdom, have decided is the correct one. Do not be that reviewer. If you are, you will soon have nothing to review. Editors will realize your incompetence as a reviewer and react accordingly.

Ideally, researchers should use *converging operations,* or a variety of methods that together converge on a given conclusion or set of conclusions about a particular psychological phenomenon. A conclusion is strengthened if multiple methodologies lead to it. Thus the goal is not to find some "right" method but, rather, to find that a number of methods all lead in the same direction.

What you should do is review an article in terms of how well it applies whatever methodology it uses, and in terms of whether the conclusions follow from the data, given the methodology or methodologies used. No article is likely to be wholly conclusive. What is important is that the author or authors recognize what they can and cannot, however much they might wish to, conclude.

Methodology may seem like one of the boring aspects of an article to which to pay attention. But arguably it is the most important. If the methods of a study are inadequate, then the results, no matter how interesting, will not hold up. A study cannot yield compelling data if the methods were not adequate to the questions being investigated. Hence, methods are key to the publishability of an article.

At the same time, reviewers can become so attuned to methods that they lose the forest for the trees. Remember that methods, although important, are not the be-all and end-all of an article. Especially in new areas of research, adequate methods may just be forming. Reviewers typically are more forgiving in a brand-new area of research than one in which the paradigms are highly developed. But if the methods are inadequate, the study probably will not be publishable, no matter how new the area of research.

When you review, be constructive. If there are methodological flaws, point them out, but also point out how the methods could be improved. Investigators can often conduct follow-up studies that correct methodological weaknesses of earlier studies, and thereby turn articles that are not publishable into ones that are. As a reviewer, your job is not just to be critical but to be a constructive critic who helps the author or authors of an article improve on the work they have done in the submitted article, in future articles, or ideally, in both.

Authors sometimes remember, over a period of years, referees who helped them improve the methodologies by which they studied the phenomena of interest to them. You can become one of those memorable referees if you give the time and effort to your review.

There are many things you need to watch out for when you review an article for methods. In this chapter, we can only begin to scratch the surface in mentioning these things.

Participants

The following is a list of questions to ask when you read about the participants in a study.

1. *Is the number of participants sufficient to generate the power needed to test the stated hypotheses?* In general, the more error variance there is in the data, the larger the N an investigator will need to be able to draw sound conclusions. The more treatment variance there is in the data, the smaller the N an investigator will need. So numbers of participants need to be evaluated relative to the variability of the data.

2. *Are the participants drawn from an appropriate population for testing?* Many researchers test college sophomores or other samples of convenience and then are rather quick to draw conclusions that extend well

beyond their sample population. You should evaluate whether the sample population is appropriate for the study and whether the conclusions are generalized to an appropriate level. For example, if someone wants to study conceptions of the nature of romantic love, testing only college sophomores might give a biased view because of the relatively limited experience such students are likely to have had with the phenomenon under investigation.

3. *Are participants balanced in ways that are relevant to the study question?* If all or most of the participants are of one kind or another, then there may be a balance problem. For example, in the study of conceptions of romantic love, it might be a problem if 80% of the sample are men (or women). If one wishes to measure a prejudice of some kind, it might be important to balance urban, suburban, and rural participants. Be sure to check for balance of participants.

4. *If the study is longitudinal, be especially aware of two issues.*

   a. *What is the dropout rate?* Conclusions of longitudinal studies can be compromised by selective dropout. Over time, participants in longitudinal studies often tend to drop out. Is the dropout rate so high as to compromise conclusions? Such a dropout rate can be especially problematic if it is selective. So ask whether there is any evidence of selective dropout, and if so, what has been done to correct for it.

   b. *Are there secular effects that might compromise conclusions?* Different age cohorts live through different experiences. For example, people born in 1920 would have lived through World War II. Those born in 1960 grew up during a time of societal ferment. Those born in 1980 have grown up in an era of widespread computer use. The point is that the experiences of different cohorts may be different, and conclusions drawn from one cohort may not be generalizable to another one. Moreover, there are secular changes in societies. For example, Flynn (1987) found that IQs rose at a rate of about 3 points per 10 years during much of the 20th century. So test norms for one testing of a cohort might not apply in a later testing.

5. *If the study is cross-sectional, be especially aware of two issues.*

   a. *Are the cohorts compared truly comparable?* Precisely because cohorts have lived through different experiences, comparisons of psychological functioning across cohorts can be fraught with danger. For example, younger participants may be at an advantage in computerized testing simply because they are more familiar with the use of computers. Older participants may be further away from their school years and hence have forgotten much of what they learned during that time and, for that reason alone, may do worse than younger cohorts on tests requiring skills learned in school.

   b. *Are the tests being used comparable for the different age groups?* If the same tests are used to ensure item comparability, then the tests may be too hard for young participants and too easy for older ones. If different tests are used, the scores on the tests simply may not be directly comparable for the different age groups. What is being done to ensure comparability?

Materials

The following are questions to ask when you read about the materials in a study.

1. *Are the materials truly appropriate for the developmental, linguistic, and cultural backgrounds of the participants being tested?* Investigators are not always sensitive to the issue of appropriateness of the materials they use. For example, materials in English may present

totally different challenges for participants whose first language is not English than for native English speakers. Sometimes the problem is not linguistic but cultural. Use of certain materials may make assumptions about cultural customs or even knowledge that is not in fact shared across cultures. For example, participants outside the United States cannot be expected to have the same knowledge of American history and geography as would participants in the United States, just as people in the United States would lack information about the history and geography of other peoples. Similarly, one needs to make sure that the materials are developmentally appropriate for the sample in the study. This consideration is especially relevant when the samples in the study are drawn from special populations (e.g., individuals with disabilities).

2. *Do participants truly understand the materials the way the investigator thinks they do?* Piaget (1972) made some seemingly reasonable but incorrect inferences from children's behavior because he assumed that the children understood the materials the way he did. For example, when asked, "Which do I have, more marbles or more green marbles?" children may become confused and give a wrong answer simply because they do not see the question as making sense. Cole, Gay, Glick, and Sharp (1971) found that Kpelle tribesmen thought that keyed answers to certain questions were stupid, whereas their own unkeyed answers were smart. They did not understand the tasks the way the investigators did. Similarly, Luria (1976) found that peasant farmers often simply refused to accept logical-reasoning problems that violated their understandings of the world.

3. *Were the materials motivating to participants, or at least, equally motivating?* Participants may fail to do well on a task because they become bored with it. Even worse, different subgroups of participants may become differentially bored, leading to results that dif-

fer across these subgroups as a result of motivation for the task rather than whatever variable is supposedly being manipulated in the study. Make sure, therefore, that motivation, and even more important, differential motivation, is not a factor underlying the results, unless that is indeed what is being studied.

4. *Were the materials adequate for representation of concepts in the study?* Make sure that materials in the study are relevant to the description of the basic study concepts in the introduction. It might be the case that the materials do not map on the concepts the author or authors discussed in the introduction. Of course, this mismatch will create difficulties for interpreting the findings; therefore, the reviewer should make sure that there is no inconsistency in the way the main concepts of the study are introduced and measured.

5. *Was the description of materials satisfactory?* It is the task of the reviewer to make sure that the description of materials in the article is clear and comprehensive. If the authors use well-known instruments and tasks, only a brief description of these instruments is warranted. However, if some or all instruments and tasks are original, then they should be described in detail so the readers can evaluate the properties of these instruments and tasks and other researchers can recreate them if needed for result verification and replication purposes.

Design

When considering design, ask yourself these questions:

1. *How were participants assigned to groups?* Was assignment random? If yes, how was randomization carried out and does this study present estimates of power conducted at the level of randomization? In

other words, if a researcher randomizes schools, are there enough schools in each group to verify the hypothesis of the study? If a researcher randomizes school districts, are there enough districts to detect the effect of interest? If not, what provisions were made, such as analysis of covariance or a pretest–posttest design, to ensure that obtained differences are not due to prior differences in groups rather than to any treatment that may have been introduced?

2. *Were there adequate control groups?* Many investigators have invested huge amounts of time in conducting investigations in which no clear conclusions could be drawn for lack of adequate control groups. For example, merely showing that a treatment improved learning from pretest to posttest is not an adequate design because participants may simply have become better at the task over time or they may show a practice effect on the posttest that has nothing to do with the treatment administered. It is not enough merely for an investigator to say he or she had a control group. As a referee, you must ensure that the comparison group adequately controlled for plausible confounding variables. If no such group appeared, then you need to ensure that adequate statistical manipulations were introduced to factor out the effects of extraneous variables. When a control group is present, it is important to make sure that treatment (experimental) and comparison (control) groups are comparable. Typically, the researchers are expected to ensure and demonstrate the comparability of treatment and comparison groups. To ensure this comparability, many researchers specify the parameters of matching (e.g., gender, age, and ethnicity) and explain how the recruitment of the comparison group was carried out. However, it is the reviewer's responsibility to verify the soundness of the research design, including the author's strategies for the recruitment of control groups or statistical control for possible confounding effects.

3. *Was the overall design well thought through?* It is important to think of all possible aspects of the design that are relevant to the data. For example, if a study is a double-blind treatment control study, then the reviewer should pay attention to precautions introduced by the author to prevent the revelation of group assignments prior to the completion of the study, especially to the individuals who work in the field. If it is an educational interventional study, an element of fidelity evaluation should be built in so that the researchers have control over how their intervention will be delivered in classrooms. If the generated data require expert judges (e.g., scoring children's compositions or drawings), make sure that the authors established reliability in evaluations.

4. *Was the dependent variable (or were the dependent variables) adequate for the hypotheses being investigated and the conclusions being drawn?* You must first ensure that the dependent variable is clearly specified. You must then make sure that it was adequate and appropriate for the hypothesis under investigation. For example, if conclusions are to be drawn about personality, was the test of personality reliable and well validated? Was it sufficiently broad to cover all personality traits that might be relevant to the questions being posed? Or, if an investigator is looking at intelligence but only uses a limited test of intelligence, can one be reasonably confident that the test measured intelligence as a whole rather than just a part of it?

5. *Are the independent variables adequate for the hypotheses being investigated and the conclusions being drawn?* First make sure that the independent variables are clearly specified. Then make sure that they correspond adequately to the underlying constructs they are supposed to represent. If they are supposed to be orthogonal, are they? Is the design clean, in the sense that it is possible to test clearly for their effects

independently of each other and in interaction? If the independent variables are correlated, what provisions have been made, such as a correlational design, to tease out their separate effects?

Procedure

The following list presents some questions to ask about the procedure.

1. *Is the procedure clearly specified?* It is essential that someone reading the study be able to understand the procedure adequately enough to be able to replicate it. If you could not replicate it on the basis of the information given, then the account is not adequate.

2. *Are there missing steps?* Sometimes investigators have weak points in their procedure that they are not eager for referees to spot. They may, intentionally or unintentionally, obfuscate certain details regarding these points of procedure. Make sure that all steps are specified without equivocation or ambiguity.

3. *Is the procedure appropriate for the participants and hypotheses being tested?* You cannot assume that the procedure is appropriate because the researcher believes it was or tries to convince you it was. It is up to you to ensure that the procedure did indeed accomplish what the investigator claims it accomplished.

4. *Is the equipment described?* Often studies require the use of particular equipment (e.g., MRI scanners, genotyping systems, or GPS devices). Make sure that all instruments essential to the work are properly described. Depending on the equipment used, results might vary from one lab to another. Therefore, all relevant machinery and all specific parameters for running this machinery should be clearly described and labeled with the manufacturer's name and location along with the model number.

5. *Was there adequate informed consent and debriefing?*
Although human-subjects committees approve almost all studies that are submitted to journals these
days, you cannot merely assume that informed
consent and debriefing were adequate. You need to
ensure that appropriate steps were taken.
6. *Was anything unethical done in the study?* Again, although a human-subjects committee probably approved the study, it is up to you to ensure that all
appropriate ethical safeguards were introduced into
the procedures of the study.
7. *Was the procedure appropriate for the ages, cultural backgrounds, or other demographic aspects of the sample or
samples being tested?* As a referee, you need to ensure
that the procedures were appropriate to the participant groups being tested. You cannot merely assume
that they were because the investigators believed
them to be.
8. *If errors were made in procedures, were they of a nature
that would fatally compromise the study?* Sometimes,
clocks stop working, computers fail, investigators
deliver the wrong stimuli to the wrong participants,
and so forth. The investigators are obligated to notify
readers of such facts. You need to ask yourself the
extent to which the study has been compromised as
a result of errors, and whether the errors might have
fatally jeopardized the study.

Hypotheses

Sometimes hypotheses are specified in the method section and
sometimes they are not. But wherever they appear, they are
potentially critical to the study. So ask yourself the following
questions.

1. *Is it clear how the hypotheses follow from whatever theory
is being offered?* Hypotheses should not merely come
out of the blue. They should fit into some theoretical

framework. Do they? And if so, do they truly follow from the theory?

2. *Are the hypotheses consistent with past data? If not, are reasons for the divergence clearly explained?* Hypotheses may or may not fit with past data. If they do, it should be made clear how they fit. If they do not, then the investigator needs clearly to explain why.

3. *Are the hypotheses plausible?* Make sure that any hypotheses presented make sense. If they do not, challenge them.

4. *Are the hypotheses interesting?* If the hypotheses are trivial, then the study may lack substance, regardless of what the findings are. So it is incumbent on you to ensure that the hypotheses are interesting and not merely trivial extensions of past work or of ideas that will make no real new contribution to the literature.

5. *Are the hypotheses mutually consistent?* Do the hypotheses fit with each other, or do any of them explicitly or implicitly contradict one another?

6. *Are the hypotheses testable?* In other words, are they framed in such a manner that they can be verified?

When you write a review, appreciate the fact that today you review someone's work and tomorrow your work will be reviewed. If you want to receive comprehensive and constructive comments when you are reviewed, make sure to be thorough and comprehensive when you review your colleagues' work!

References

Cole, M., Gay, J., Glick, J., & Sharp, D. W. (1971). *The cultural context of learning and thinking.* New York: Basic Books.

Flynn, J. R. (1987). Massive IQ gains in 14 nations. *Psychological Bulletin, 101,* 171–191.

Luria, A. R. (1976). *Cognitive development: Its cultural and social foundations.* Cambridge, MA: Harvard University Press.

Piaget, J. (1972). *The psychology of intelligence.* Totowa, NJ: Littlefield Adams.

3

Reviewing Theory Articles

Robert J. Sternberg

How does one review theory articles? Because this topic is so abstract, it may be helpful to have a concrete classic case study to serve as an example for the points to be made. The classic case study to be used is that of cognitive dissonance theory and its successor, self-perception theory. If you are familiar with this conflict, you may be able to skip the next section. But if you are fuzzy on the details, I urge you to read the case study of a classic theory, as it will serve as the basis for illustrating points in the rest of this chapter.

A Case Study

The Experiment

Imagine that you are participating in an experiment in which the experimenter asks you to perform two mind-numbingly simple tasks of eye–hand coordination. The tasks are repeatedly emptying and refilling a tray that contains spools of thread for half an hour, and then repeatedly turning an array of pegs one-quarter turn each for another half an hour. After you have performed these excruciatingly dull tasks for a full hour, the experimenter mercifully tells you that you may stop. As far as you know, that is the end of the experiment on eye–hand coordination.

Now, as is customary after a psychological experiment, the experimenter debriefs you. He explains that the purpose of the experiment was to investigate the effects of psychological mind-set on task performance. You were in the control group, so you were given no prior indication of whether the tasks would be interesting. In the experimental group, on the other hand, participants were told in advance that the tasks would be enjoyable. The experimenter goes on to tell you that the next participant, who is waiting outside, has been assigned to the experimental group. A research assistant will arrive soon to tell her how great the task will be.

Then the experimenter leaves the room for a moment and returns, worried because his research assistant has not yet arrived. Would you be willing to salvage the experiment by serving as a paid research assistant just for this one participant? Persuaded, you tell the next participant how much fun the experiment was. She replies that she had heard from a friend that it was a bore. You assure her, however, that it was pure entertainment. Then you depart. As you leave, a secretary in the psychology department interviews you briefly. She asks you to rate just how much fun and how interesting the experiment really was.

The independent variable was not whether you were told in advance that the experiment was fun and interesting. In fact, you and all the other participants who believed you were in the "control" condition were actually in the experimental condition. In the genuine control condition, participants merely performed the boring tasks and later were asked how interesting the tasks were.

In the true experimental condition in this classic study by Festinger and Carlsmith (1959), the "participant" waiting outside was a confederate of the experimenter. There never was any other research assistant: The plan had always been to get you to convince the next "participant" that the experiment was a delight. The crucial manipulation was the amount of money you received for saying that the experiment was interesting. The independent variable actually was that some participants were paid only $1; other participants were paid $20. The dependent variable was the experimental participant's rating of the interest level of the tasks when questioned by the secretary. The goal was to find out whether a relationship existed between the amount of money a person was paid for lying about the tasks and how interesting the person later reported the dull tasks to be. In other words, how did lying about tasks affect people's attitudes toward those tasks?

Participants who were paid $1 rated the boring experiment as much more interesting than did either those who were paid $20 or the control participants. This result came as a great shock to the field of psychology. The existing incentive motivation theory predicted that individuals in the $20 group would have much more incentive to change their attitude toward the experiment than would individuals in the $1 group because $20 was a much greater reward. Hence, this theory predicted that people in the $20 group would be much more motivated to show, and actually would show, more attitude change (Hovland, Janis, & Kelley, 1953). Festinger and Carlsmith (1959) explained the counter-intuitive results by suggesting that the participants' responses could be understood in terms of their efforts to achieve cognitive consistency, the match between a person's thoughts and behaviors. The fundamental importance of cognitive consistency was first pointed out by Fritz Heider (1958), who recognized that when people's cognitions are inconsistent, people strive to restore consistency. Cognitive consistency is extremely important to our mental well-being. Without it, we feel tense, nervous, irritable, and even at war with ourselves.

Now let us think about why people in the $1 group showed more attitude change. Two possible explanations are found in cognitive dissonance theory and self-perception theory.

Two Theories to Account for the Results of the Experiment

Cognitive Dissonance Theory. Let us reconsider the Festinger and Carlsmith (1959) experiment: The participants who were paid $20 performed an extremely boring task and then encouraged someone else to believe that the task was interesting. They were well compensated for doing so, however. They achieved cognitive consistency easily. Saying that a dull task was interesting but getting paid well for saying so allowed these participants to match their thoughts and beliefs to their behavior.

Now consider the plight of the participants who were paid $1. They not only performed a boring task but also lied about it by trying to convince someone else that it was interesting. Furthermore, they were paid poorly for their efforts. These participants may have been experiencing cognitive dissonance, the disquieting perception of a mismatch among one's own attitudes.

Justification of effort—a means by which an individual rationalizes his or her expenditure of energy—is one route to reducing cognitive dissonance. Most of us need to feel that we have good, logical reasons for why we do what we do. But how could the poorly paid experimental participants justify their efforts on the task? The only apparent justification was to decide that perhaps it was not really so bad. After all, it would have been embarrassing to admit that not only had they not liked the task but also they had lied about it to someone else and then had been paid only a small amount of money for doing so. How much easier it must have been to decide that maybe it was all worth it. Perhaps the task was even interesting and enjoyable. Thus, these latter participants reduced cognitive dissonance by deciding that the task was perfectly acceptable. They made sense of the lies they had told the confederate by deceiving themselves and changing their attitude toward the boring task.

We now look more closely at the conditions under which cognitive dissonance occurs. Dissonance is most likely to occur when (a) you have freely chosen the action that causes the dissonance; (b) you have firmly committed yourself to that behavior, and the commitment or behavior is irrevocable; and (c) your behavior has significant consequences for other people. Suppose that a couple is very unhappily married and they have children. Both parents devoutly believe that divorce is morally wrong, especially when a couple has children. This is a classic situation likely to generate cognitive dissonance.

In contrast, you are less likely to experience cognitive dissonance if you are forced into an action, if you still have the option of not continuing to perform the action, or if your behavior has consequences for no one but you. Someone who is coerced into marriage or who has no children to think about may have less compunction about filing for divorce. This interpretation of the Festinger and Carlsmith (1959) experiment is only one of several. Consider now the rather different analysis of self-perception theory, which describes another route to cognitive consistency.

Self-Perception Theory. If questioned about the connection between our beliefs and our behavior, most of us would probably say that our behavior is caused by our beliefs. An influential theory suggests the opposite (Bem, 1967, 1972). According to self-perception theory, when we are not sure of what we believe, we infer our beliefs from our behavior. We perceive our own actions much as an outside observer would. We draw conclusions about ourselves on the basis on our actions.

Consider how self-perception theory would interpret the Festinger and Carlsmith (1959) experiment. As you find yourself explaining to another participant how enjoyable the experiment was, you wonder, "Why in the world am I doing this?" If you have been paid $20, the explanation is easy: for the money. If you have been paid only $1, however, you cannot be doing it for the money. So a logical interpretation is that you must have liked the task.

Self-perception influences your attitudes in other circumstances as well. To return to an earlier example, suppose you are trying to figure out whether you want to become more involved with someone. You realize that you have been spending a lot of time with the person, exchanging gifts, and spending much less time with friends. You infer on the basis of your behavior that you must really care a great deal about this person. You decide you must be ready for a deeper commitment.

It can be advantageous to consider whether our entrenched self-perceptions may unnecessarily limit our options. People change, preferences change, and fears change. According to self-perception theory, when we behave in a way that conflicts with our habitual reactions, we have a chance to look at ourselves from a fresh perspective. We may just change our self-perceptions and change how we behave.

Cognitive Dissonance Versus Self-Perception Theory. Re-searchers have conducted experiments to determine whether cognitive dissonance or self-perception theory better explains behavior that contradicts prior beliefs (e.g., Bem, 1967; Cooper, Zanna, & Taves, 1978). What are the results?

It appears that cognitive dissonance theory applies better when people behave in ways that do not agree with their usual beliefs or attitudes. Suppose you have always been a staunch believer in one point of view. But a friend convinces you to attend meetings of an opposing group, which you then find persuasive. Your lack of cognitive consistency might bear out dissonance theory.

Thus, cognitive dissonance theory seems to explain attitude change better, particularly when the change is dramatic and the original beliefs and attitudes were obvious and well defined. Self-perception theory seems to explain attitude formation better, when the person's attitudes are still ambivalent (Fazio, Zanna, & Cooper, 1977). It applies better when people behave in ways that are only slightly discrepant from their normal patterns, particularly when the attitudes are vague, uncertain, and not fully formed.

What to Look for in Reviewing Theory Articles

When you review theory articles, I believe there are 12 critical criteria to evaluate. They are (a) sufficient clarity and detail, (b) original substantive contribution, (c) relation to previous work, (d) explanatory value, (e) falsifiability, (f) generalizability, (g) dis-criminability, (h) internal consistency, (i) external correspondence to past data (postdictive validity), (j) external correspondence to future data (predictive validity), (k) parsimony, and (l) excite-ment. The Festinger and Carlsmith (1959) study is close to a paragon on most, if not all, of these dimensions.

Clarity and Detail

Some theories are specified in so little detail or with so little clarity that it is hard to know exactly what they are saying. At times it is difficult to know even what the theory is. For example, some theorists have, from time to time, discussed the possibility of an "existential" intelligence or a "spiritual" intelligence (e.g., Gardner, 1999). Is there such a thing? Maybe. But it will be hard to know unless the theorists specify what such constructs mean in sufficient detail and with sufficient clarity that one can figure out just what they are claiming.

In contrast, Festinger and Carlsmith's (1959) theory of cognitive dissonance was specified in some detail and with considerable precision. Researchers were able to design hundreds of studies to test the theory under diverse circumstances because they knew just what they were testing.

Uncomfortably for theorists, the more precisely they specify their theories, the more likely they are to find the theory disconfirmed, usually by someone other than themselves. The goal of science is not to specify theories that are "correct," but rather to specify theories that will give way to successor theories that are, hopefully, better than the ones they replace. Precision in specification of a theory enables other researchers to design tests of the theory and thereby to advance science beyond where it is.

Sometimes theories are quite complex and seem to resist easy understanding. If you read the terms of the theory more than once and still do not understand them, you should not assume that the problem is with you. In your review, you should ask the author or authors to explain the theory more clearly. The obligation is on the writer to make things clear, not on the reader to puzzle them out.

Original Substantive Contribution

Festinger and Carlsmith's (1959) theory was like a bombshell dropped on the field of psychology, in general, and social psychology, in particular. The result of Festinger and Carlsmith was strange enough: $1 resulted in more attitude change than $20! Their theory of cognitive dissonance explained this finding, which until then, would not have fit any existing theoretical framework.

In reviewing a theoretical article, it is essential that you know or survey the literature carefully to evaluate the original contribution of the new theory you are evaluating. Top theoretical journals such as *Psychological Review* generally will be interested in a theory only if it goes well beyond what past theories have had to offer. Other theoretical journals as well will expect contributions to be original.

Original theoretical contributions can be of several different kinds (Sternberg, 1999b).

1. *Replication.* The theory is an attempt to show that the field is in the right place. A replicative theory basically is a minor variant of past theories and is unlikely to find a place in a top theory journal.

2. *Redefinition.* The theory is an attempt to redefine where the field is. The current status of the field thus is seen from different points of view.

3. *Forward incrementation.* The theory is an attempt to move the field forward in the direction it is already going.

4. *Advance forward incrementation.* The contribution is an attempt to move the field forward in the direction it is already going, but by moving beyond where others are ready for it to go.

5. *Redirection.* The contribution is an attempt to redirect the field from where it is toward a different direction.

6. *Reconstruction or redirection.* The contribution is an attempt to move the field back to where it once was (a reconstruction of the past) so that it may move onward from that point, but in a direction different from the one it took from that point onward.

7. *Reinitiation.* The contribution is an attempt to move the field to a different as yet unreached starting point and then to move from that point.

8. *Integration.* The contribution is an attempt to integrate two formerly diverse ways of thinking about phenomena into a single way of thinking about a phenomenon.

The eight types of creative contributions described above are largely qualitatively distinct. Within each type, however, there can be quantitative differences. For example, a forward incrementation can represent a fairly small step forward or a substantial leap. A reinitiation can restart a subfield (e.g., Festinger and Carlsmith's work on cognitive dissonance) or an entire field (e.g., the work of Einstein on relativity theory). Thus, the theory distinguishes contributions both qualitatively and quantitatively.

Relation to Past Work

All theories, no matter how novel, build on past work. Indeed, they should build on past work. A theory article that fails to cite the work on which it was built is defective, no matter how original it is. As noted above, there are different ways of building on past work. But science is a cumulative enterprise, and so theorists must make it clear how their new theory is similar to and different from past theories. Even Newton referred to himself as "standing on the shoulders of giants." The article should make clear what past theories have said, what the present theory says, and how the present theory is similar to and different from the past theories.

It should also state explicitly what unresolved issues from past work led to its formulation. Typically, there are three ways in which old work breeds new.

1. Past theories could not account for subsequent data.
2. Past theories actually did not account for old data as well as it first appeared they did.
3. Past theories, for whatever questions they answered, nevertheless left important questions unanswered. When new questions are asked, it is usually because
   a. new methodologies have enabled investigators to ask questions that they previously could not have asked, and
   b. new paradigms for understanding a phenomenon (e.g., cognitivism or connectionism) elucidated issues that previously had not been dealt with, or at least had not been dealt with adequately.

One thing reviewers must be sensitive to is literature reviews that are standard discussions of issues but that do not really illuminate the new theory being presented. The literature review should form a part of a story, where it recounts the earlier parts of the story, and the new theory recounts the later parts. For example, Bem (1967), in presenting self-perception theory, showed that although cognitive dissonance theory answered some questions, it failed to answer others.

Falsifiability

Popper (1959) argued that the principal basis for scientific progress is falsification. A good theory is one that is falsifiable. A good scientist, from this point of view, presents a theory that can be falsified, and indeed, deliberately designs experiments to falsify his or her own theory. In practice, other investigators are more likely to be the ones who falsify the theory.

It is not enough to state that a theory is falsifiable. The author of a theory paper should state particular empirical predictions the theory makes that, if they were to come to be, would falsify the theory.

One type of theoretical presentation shows selected past facts that are consistent with the theory. Such a presentation is somewhat problematical. For example, Gardner (1983) and Carroll (1993) presented voluminous data from past work that they argued was consistent with their theories. Each wrote a rather lengthy book describing supporting evidence. The problem is that their theories are, to a large extent, mutually incompatible. At the highest level, Carroll's theory posits a general ability as at the apex of a hierarchical framework for understanding intelligence. Gardner posits the absence of a general ability, and a set of multiple intelligences of equal, rather than hierarchically arranged, levels of importance. How could such an inconsistency emerge? The answer is simple: Authors tend to review in detail evidence that is consistent with their theory and to ignore or discount evidence that is inconsistent with their theory. As a reviewer, it is your responsibility to make sure that the literature is reasonably balanced and that it highlights past theories and data that are consistent as well as inconsistent with the newly proposed theory.

Bem (1972) designed elegant experiments to falsify the theory of cognitive dissonance. He was apparently successful, at least to some extent, and for a while his self-perception theory seemed to be on the verge of replacing dissonance theory. But then others showed that his theory did not hold up under all circumstances, which led investigators to seek the circumstances under which self-perception might apply and the other circumstances under which cognitive dissonance might apply.

This kind of dialectical progression is commonplace in science. Hegel (1931/1807) proposed that thought generally proceeds in this fashion. First there is a thesis. Then there is a seemingly contradictory antithesis. Finally there is some kind of thesis that points out how the seemingly incompatible ideas can be integrated, at least at some level. This synthesis then becomes the basis for a new thesis (see Sternberg, 1999a).

The most compelling kind of demonstration of the validity of a theory is one that uses converging operations (Garner, Hake, & Eriksen, 1956), whereby different kinds of methodologies are used to demonstrate the validity of a theory. For example, one might test the theory of cognitive dissonance in laboratory experiments or in experiments studying people in everyday life, across cultures, developmentally for children of different ages, and so forth.

Why do we speak of falsifiability of a theory rather than verifiability? The reason is that one can never fully verify a theory. Theory verification is inductive. One can show that a theory works under one set of circumstances, and then under another set of circumstances, and then under still another set of circumstances.

Generalizability

One can never show a theory that works under all circumstances, any more than one can prove that all ravens are black. There is always the possibility that the next raven one examines will be any color but black. Typically, in psychology, theories apply under a set of circumstances, but not all circumstances. It is important that the theorist state clearly those circumstances under which the theory is expected to apply and those under which it is not. Testing large numbers of college sophomores in labs and showing that the theory holds up under these conditions typically does not show the conditions under which a theory applies or does not apply.

Some theorists do not treat the question of generalizability seriously. They assume that if a theory can be shown to hold in a limited sample with a limited set of empirical operations under a limited set of circumstances, that is enough. The problem is that this assumption is one only of convenience, not of reality. Cultural researchers have found that very different patterns of behavior may occur in different cultures (e.g., Greenfield, 1997; Nisbett, 2003; Serpell, 2000; Sternberg, 2004). Merely avoiding the inconvenience of testing across cultures does not make the issue go away.

Cognitive dissonance theory was remarkably, although not fully, generalizable. It was tested under many circumstances. When it did not hold up under all circumstances, it was not a disaster for the theory. On the contrary, the goal of empirical research is to discover the limitations of all theories, dissonance theory included.

Discriminability

It might seem that the more a theory can account for, the better the theory is. This notion is probably true, up to a point. But a theory that can account for too much, in essence, can account for nothing at all. It is important, in reviewing theory articles, to look for a statement by the author or authors of the theory's boundaries—where it stops and what it cannot account for. If it is presented as the universal theory of everything, chances are that it is actually a theory of nothing.

For example, it was not clear in the initial presentation of cognitive dissonance theory what its limits were—that cognitive dissonance applied better to attitude change than to attitude formation. This relative limitation of the theory emerged over time. Typically, theorists do not realize when they first present their theory what its limitations are. But they are obliged at the very least to speculate, and thereby to suggest to other researchers, areas of investigation for testing the theory.

Internal Consistency

A theory needs to be internally consistent. Internal consistency requires that no aspect of the theory be inconsistent with any other aspect. In other words, its parts should cohere. This requirement might seem like a minor one, but as anyone knows who has ever tried to implement a theory on a computer, it is not. It is difficult, in many instances, to get the theory operationalized in a way that results in the program's running and yielding sensible output. Cognitive dissonance theory was internally consistent, and thus passed this important test.

External Correspondence to Past Data (Postdictive Validity)

Theory papers typically consist of a section in which the theorist attempts to show that his or her theory postdicts past data—that is, the theory is consistent with as much data previously collected as possible. Carroll (1993), in presenting a so-called three-strata theory of human intelligence, reanalyzed hundreds of past data sets to show that his theory was consistent with findings from earlier investigations. Similarly, the theory of cognitive dissonance was attractive in part because it seemed to explain attitude change in ways that existing theories at the time could not do.

The problem with postdictive demonstrations is usually selective presentation of data. For example, Carroll (1993) reanalyzed past data sets, but they were all psychometric data sets susceptible to factor analysis. This set of data was compatible with his goals but may have omitted data relevant to the problem of how intelligence is structured that were not susceptible to factor analysis. So in evaluating the postdictive validity of a theory, it is important to assess the extent to which it accounts for representative data, not those that are merely selected to represent data of a particular kind or that represent a certain kind of finding.

When Festinger and Carlsmith (1959) presented their results, incentive motivation theory was in its prime. And it seemed to be accounting for existing data. What these investigators did was to design a new paradigm to show the limitations of the theory—that in a particular situation, the result obtained was the opposite of that predicted by incentive motivation theory. Their result seemed to require a new theory that could account for past data (it did) and new data as well (it did, at the time).

External Correspondence to Future Data (Prediction)

The most impressive kind of empirical validation of a theory is that which predicts data not yet collected at the time the theory is proposed. Such a demonstration of predictive validity is impressive because the reader knows that the theory was not created after the fact to account post hoc for data already collected. The more data the theory can predict, and the more diverse those data are, the more compelling is the demonstrated validity of the theory. Cognitive dissonance theory eventually was found to predict some, but not all, data.

Parsimony

Parsimony probably receives less attention today than it did in the past. Yet it remains one of the criteria by which theories are judged. If two theories predict the same data, or at least the same amount of data, and one is more parsimonious than the other, then investigators will generally be inclined to prefer the more parsimonious theory. Theories that are weighted down with many complexities tend to be less attractive, in part, because it can become so difficult to test them in all of their complexity, or even to be clear on how one would test them. Cognitive dissonance theory was quite parsimonious, and moreover, rested on what seemed to be plausible and simple intuitions about human nature.

Excitement

The criterion of excitement differs in kind from the other criteria in the sense that reviewers might not explicitly state that, in the end, they were reluctant to recommend accepting a theory article because it was so boring. But in science, as in art and literature, excitement counts. Some articles become widely cited, others less so, in large part because of the excitement they generate. The researchers who are most visible in the field generally are those whose work generates the greatest amount of excitement within their field of interest, and sometimes, outside their field as well.

Few people do cognitive dissonance research anymore. The days of the theory have come and gone. Excitement is an ephemeral construct. This is all to the good, as inevitably a field must move on.

Conclusion

In this chapter, I have briefly reviewed criteria by which theory articles can be evaluated: (a) sufficient clarity and detail, (b) original substantive contribution, (c) relation to previous work, (d) explanatory value, (e) falsifiability, (f) generalizability, (g) discriminability, (h) internal consistency, (i) external correspondence to past data (postdictive validity), (j) external correspondence to future data (predictive validity), (k) parsimony, and (l) excitement. I make no claim that these criteria are exhaustive or even, in all cases, mutually exclusive. But theory articles tend to be better when they strive to meet these 12 criteria. Look for them when you review theoretical articles.

References

Bem, D. J. (1967). Self-perception: An alternative interpretation of cognitive dissonance phenomena. *Psychological Review, 74,* 183–200.

Bem, D. J. (1972). Self-perception theory. In L. Berkowitz (Ed.), *Advances in experimental social psychology* (Vol. 6, pp. 1–62). New York: Academic Press.

Carroll, J. B. (1993). *Human cognitive abilities: A survey of factor-analytic studies.* New York: Cambridge University Press.

Cooper, J., Zanna, M. P., & Taves, P. A. (1978). Arousal as a necessary condition for attitude change following induced compliance. *Journal of Personality and Social Psychology, 36,* 1101–1106.

Fazio, R. H., Zanna, M. P., & Cooper, J. (1977). Dissonance and self perception: An integrative view of each theory's proper domain of application. *Journal of Experimental Social Psychology, 13,* 464–479.

Festinger, L., & Carlsmith, J. M. (1959). Cognitive consequences of forced compliance. *Journal of Abnormal and Social Psychology, 58,* 203–210.

Gardner, H. (1983). *Frames of mind: The theory of multiple intelligences.* New York: Basic.

Gardner, H. (1999). Are there additional intelligences? The case for naturalist, spiritual, and existential intelligences. In J. Kane (Ed.), *Education, information, and transformation* (pp. 111–131). Upper Saddle River, NJ: Prentice-Hall.

Garner, W. R., Hake, H. W., & Eriksen, C. W. (1956). Operationism and the concept of perception. *Psychological Review, 63,* 149–159.

Greenfield, P. M. (1997). You can't take it with you: Why abilities assessments don't cross cultures. *American Psychologist, 52,* 1115–1124.

Hegel, G. W. F. (1931). *The phenomenology of the mind* (2nd ed.; J. B. Baillie, Trans.). London: Allen & Unwin. (Original work published 1807)

Heider, F. (1958). *The psychology of interpersonal relations.* New York: Wiley.

Hovland, C. I., Janis, I. L., & Kelley, H. H. (1953). *Communication and persuasion: Psychological studies of opinion change.* New Haven, CT: Yale University Press.

Nisbett, R. E. (2003). *The geography of thought: Why we think the way we do.* New York: The Free Press.

Popper, K. R. (1959). *The logic of scientific discovery.* London: Hutchinson.

Serpell, R. (2000). Intelligence and culture. In R. J. Sternberg (Ed.), *Handbook of intelligence* (pp. 549–580). New York: Cambridge University Press.

Sternberg, R. J. (1999a). A dialectical basis for understanding the study of cognition. In R. J. Sternberg (Ed.), *The nature of cognition* (pp. 51–78). Cambridge, MA: MIT Press.

Sternberg, R. J. (1999b). A propulsion model of types of creative contributions. *Review of General Psychology, 3,* 83–100.

Sternberg, R. J. (2004). Culture and intelligence. *American Psychologist. 59,* 325–338.

4

Refereeing Literature Review Submissions to Journals

Alice H. Eagly

Referees of potential journal articles have a dual responsibility. They are both enforcers of standards and teachers devoted to improving the quality of journal articles and developing the talents of researchers. As enforcers of standards, referees provide the peer review that is essential to maintaining high quality in the scientific literature. Referees must themselves be highly qualified as researchers and scholars to be able to appropriately enforce high standards as referees of literature reviews as well as of other types of journal articles. As teachers, they should instruct authors in the processes that are needed to improve their manuscripts sufficiently that they may become publishable. Both of these jobs become easier as the quality of submitted manuscripts improves. The task of enforcing standards is easy if a manuscript meets or even surpasses reasonable standards. And the authors of a high-quality manuscript may need little instruction.

Serving as a referee of reviews of the literature is a weighty responsibility because reviews have the potential to become important statements that define scientific knowledge in a research area. The publication of an article that reviews and integrates a substantial body of knowledge is a signal achievement in a scholar's career, given the influence that such articles can have.

On average, individual reviews are more influential than individual research articles, precisely because they offer general conclusions about groups of studies—sometimes very large numbers of studies. It is thus not surprising that the publications in psychology with the highest *impact factor*, defined as the average number of citations per article, are psychology's best known outlets for publishing reviews: *Annual Review of Psychology* and *Psychological Bulletin* (ISI Journal Citation Reports, 2005). Articles in these two publications have a higher impact factor even than articles in *Psychological Review*, the highest status journal for publishing theoretical articles.

Reviews distill research findings into generalizations, sometimes complex and sometimes simple, that are cited not only in subsequent research articles but also in textbooks and trade books presenting research to wider audiences. Therefore, it is extremely important that literature reviews accurately represent research findings. To ensure this outcome, referees of literature reviews must be skillful, fair, and very attentive to the manuscript at all levels ranging from its overall purposes and method to the details of its findings. In addition, referees must be energetic and even a bit courageous to undertake the demanding task of evaluating a substantial review manuscript. Because these manuscripts are often long and complex, it can be difficult to restrain the sinking feeling that can accompany printing out one of these large manuscripts, which are now generally delivered to the referee as an e-mail attachment. The referee may have to break out a new ream of paper to finish the printing job and find a heavy metal clip to keep the printed pages together. It is unlikely that the referee can complete the evaluation of such a manuscript without devoting several hours to the task.

It is also possible for a referee to feel quite humble when contemplating this task if the manuscript is potentially a major contribution to the scholarly literature. To be fully adequate as a referee, an individual might ideally have considerable expertise in the specific topic of the review, and, in the case of meta-analyses, considerable technical expertise in meta-analysis. However, referees should assume that the journal editor has invited them because they possess relevant expertise in some important aspect of the manuscript. Sometimes a journal editor recruits referees who represent differing perspectives or differing competencies. One individual may be invited to referee because of specific content expertise, another because of wide experience in the general domain of the review, and still another mainly because of technical competence in meta-analysis. If referees are not knowledgeable in relation to all facets of a manuscript, they can frankly acknowledge in their evaluation that they were attentive mainly to certain aspects of the manuscript and made less effort to evaluate certain other aspects that did not fully lie within their competence.

Of course, the effort that goes into refereeing such a manuscript is very small compared with the effort of producing the manuscript. Because of the authors' efforts, referees should be respectful of the authors' dedication to their task. Nonetheless, it is not uncommon that a psychologist who undertakes a literature review does not initially realize how demanding such a project will be or how large a commitment of time and effort it will require. Significant reviews generally require not just months of effort but effort spread over 1, 2, 3, or even more years. Scholars' understandable desire to move fairly quickly to the goal of publishing a review can lead them to submit reviews that are underdeveloped. An experienced referee will detect the ways in which the project would benefit from more development. In providing feedback to the author, referees should react in part to the goals of the project and ask themselves whether the review could become an important contribution if it were developed further. If the project seems worthy, the task of refereeing an initial submission to a journal generally becomes one of providing guidance that helps the author to develop the project. Therefore, given a potentially informative project, referees, like good teachers, should adopt a positive tone in their feedback and encourage the authors. Referees need to hold out hope that the authors can develop the project to the point that it will be published in a good journal. Referees should point the way toward a stronger review.

Types of Reviews

The referee's task differs, depending on the type of review that he or she is evaluating (Cooper, 2003). With respect to the overall focus of a review, the most common type integrates empirical findings on a given topic, often on a specific hypothesis. Although it is possible to consider articles not focusing on empirical findings to constitute reviews because the articles focus on research methods or theories, such articles would more properly be considered methodological or theoretical contributions. Therefore, good practices in refereeing them are considered in other chapters of this book.

The goal of a review of empirical findings is to determine what generalizations the available findings yield about the phenomena investigated. For example, if the question were whether women and men differ in aggressiveness, the reviewer (i.e., the author of the review) would have located a body of studies that compared the sexes on measures of aggressiveness (e.g., Bettencourt & Miller, 1996). The domain of studies relevant to aggressiveness could be defined narrowly, perhaps by encompassing only experimental studies, or more broadly, by including, for example, studies of violent crime and family violence. Very broad definitions are, however, unlikely in a journal article, given that such a review would have to cover several very large groups of studies. Therefore, a subdomain such as sex differences in aggression in partner relationships would generally merit its own review (e.g., Archer, 2000). Reviewers of aggression studies of any type would ordinarily be interested not only in producing a general conclusion about the male–female comparison but also in finding out why the comparisons sometimes yield larger differences and sometimes yield smaller or reversed differences.

Even within the domain of manuscripts that review empirical findings, there is considerable variability in reviewers' goals. Most commonly, integrations of empirical findings are mainly intended to produce generalizations about a phenomenon, but sometimes findings are reviewed to criticize a research domain, identify its central issues, or test a theory (Cooper, 2003). When criticism, issue identification, or theory testing is a review's main goal, it is less likely that a reviewer has attempted to identify all potentially relevant studies. Instead, studies (or sometimes other reviews) are used to illustrate the reviewer's major points. In this chapter, most of the attention is devoted to reviews that do have as their main purpose the integration of research findings to produce generalizations about specific phenomena.

To integrate the findings of a group of studies, reviewers may proceed with quantitative methods, producing a quantitative synthesis or meta-analysis. Alternatively, reviewers may eschew quantitative methods, producing a narrative review. The narrative form of review is especially useful in the beginning stage of a research tradition, when very few studies are available and these studies can be summarized individually. Reviews of this type are often found in the introductions to journal articles presenting primary research. In more developed research traditions in which many studies exist, meta-analysis is ordinarily the method of choice, particularly if reviews are confined to specific hypotheses. Meta-analyses thus integrate findings pertaining to a single hypothesis or a group of closely related hypotheses. Meta-analyses appear in scholarly journals that are read mainly by researchers, professors, and graduate students, who typically have the statistical training to comprehend such a project. However, when reviewers have broader purposes of integrating across many hypotheses that have been active within a research area, quantitative methods are usually not feasible, although reviewers may rely on existing meta-analyses as components of their broad overview. Narrative reviews are also common in areas in which research findings are often not quantified or, when they are quantified, very diverse methods would make the findings noncomparable. Also, when a review is intended to be read by the general public or by undergraduate students, reviewers generally do not proceed with quantitative methods.

In the discussion that follows, my comments are confined to refereeing literature reviews that are submitted to scholarly journals. First I consider criteria for evaluation that are relevant to all such reviews, and then I separately consider quantitative syntheses and narrative reviews.

Criteria That Are Relevant
to All Empirical Reviews

A sound review article has well-formulated goals and a clear domain of coverage. Referees search for these attributes in their initial look at a manuscript. These features should be explained in the beginning pages of the manuscript. If the goals and domain of the manuscript appear to be overly diffuse (e.g., reviewing research on altruism), the manuscript would not make a good impression on the referee. The domain of altruism studies might be appropriate for a book with many chapters, but surely not for a journal article.

The introduction to a review provides a conceptual overview and analysis of the reviewed literature. The referee would examine this analysis for the adequacy of its definition of the phenomena that the review summarizes and integrates. Key terms should be introduced and defined, major theoretical approaches outlined, and the conduct of typical studies described. The referee evaluates whether this introductory conceptual analysis tells readers what they need to know to understand the remainder of the manuscript. These introductory pages should be accessible to a wide range of research psychologists and graduate students in psychology if the intended outlet of the article is a general psychology journal such as *Psychological Bulletin*. A manuscript submitted to a more specialized journal can assume considerably more specialized background on the part of the typical reader. The referee thus should keep the audience of the potential journal article in mind in evaluating whether the author has provided an adequate amount of background information in the paper.

After determining the author's definition of the goals and domain of the manuscript in the abstract and introductory pages, the referee likely would scan the manuscript to determine how it is organized. Often the organization is explained toward the end of the introductory pages, and, if not, the organization can ordinarily be discerned by scanning the headings and subheadings that appear throughout the manuscript. A referee would justifiably be discouraged if the organization of the manuscript could not be easily discovered. This organization should give the manuscript a logical progression that carries readers along through the questions and subquestions that reveal the contents of the empirical literature in the identified domain.

The referee's preliminary scan of the manuscript might move quickly from the abstract, the introduction, and the section headings to the conclusion of the review to discern whether the author has produced a take-home message that is interesting or provocative enough that the review likely will attract readers and potentially be influential. Just what type of readers should be attracted depends on the particular journal to which the manuscript has been submitted. For a review journal such as *Psychological Bulletin* that serves psychology as a whole, the conclusions of the manuscript should be interesting to an audience that goes well beyond those researchers who specialize in the same research area. However, for a more specialized journal, such as *Personality and Social Psychology Review*, a narrower audience may be the intended target of the article.

In summary, when beginning the evaluation of a review manuscript, the referee would be well advised to start by taking the manuscript in hand and scanning it for its goals, organization, and conclusions. The referee then proceeds to the hard work of carefully studying the detailed content of the manuscript to determine if the authors' goals are achieved and conclusions justified. Of course, it may occasionally happen that the preliminary scan reveals such serious deficits (e.g., diffuse goals, unclear definition of the scope of the empirical literature) that the referee is justified in forgoing truly careful study of the details of the manuscript. Usually, however, the review has the potential to become a valuable contribution to the scholarly literature—if not in the form that it was submitted to the journal, then in a more developed revised manuscript.

Referee Criteria That Are Relevant Mainly to Meta-Analyses

Meta-analyses present referees with the task of evaluating a host of technical and statistical issues in addition to broader issues such as the presence of well-articulated goals and conclusions. The organization of a meta-analysis is for the most part straightforward because it consists of the same four general sections as an empirical article—that is, introduction, method, results, and discussion. Therefore, after first skimming the manuscript as a whole and then studying the introduction in some detail, the referee moves on to the method section.

Evaluating the Method of Meta-Analyses

In my experience as a referee of many reviews, most meta-analyses are deficient in their method when they are first submitted to a journal. These deficiencies can occasionally be detected in the detailed setting of the boundaries of the research literature. These boundaries can be vaguely stated or perhaps are not defended or defensible. When the boundaries are clear, the reviewers usually imply that they intend to locate the entire research literature within these boundaries.

Despite the reviewer's intention of accessing an entire research literature, often the method of the review yields little chance of finding all of the available studies. For example, if the authors state that they confined their search to published literature, they would not find the entire literature. Such a decision should be defended so that readers will not conclude that this decision produced a bias in favor of the hypothesis that follows from the difficulties of publishing nonconfirming studies (Greenwald, 1975). The fact that published studies are easier to access is not a sufficient reason, especially in view of the ease with which unpublished dissertations can be located in the online version of *Dissertation Abstracts International*. Confining the search to articles written in English is also difficult to defend, for similar reasons. All too often reviewers have set arbitrary boundaries that probably produce bias in their conclusions (e.g., only published studies reported in English). Therefore, a responsible referee advises the authors of the review to backtrack and search the omitted domains.

Another practice often observed in submitted manuscripts is that the authors have confined their electronic searching to PsycINFO. Although this database is very large and likely to reach most studies published in psychology journals, searching in this database is generally not sufficient. Many other databases may contain relevant articles. Depending on the topic of the review, databases such as ERIC (Educational Resources Information Center), ABI/Inform, and MEDLINE can be consulted. There are multiple databases covering literature published in other nations, including dissertations. Moreover, for seminal articles in a field, Web of Science allows reviewers to use the descendancy approach, which involves locating all of the articles that cited particular articles. When only one database is noted in the method section of the review (and perhaps even this one database has been searched with a limited number of keywords), the referee should call for the reviewers to be more thorough. The referee might even spend a few minutes checking out what references would come up in databases not cited by the reviewers. In the case of a manuscript that I refereed not long ago, a 10-minute period of searching quickly revealed at least 200 apparently eligible articles that had been omitted from the review. The author appeared to have used his own files and a very minimal PsycINFO search as the source of the relevant literature, and the result was a massively underinclusive database.

Referees should be especially impressed by evidence that the authors of a review attempted to locate unpublished studies, especially if the research area is currently active and therefore many projects may be in progress or under review. A common method is to post notices on multiple electronic mailing lists that are likely to reach researchers in the area. Conference programs can also be perused, and reviewers can send inquiries to active investigators.

The referee expects to read not just a description of the searching method but a description of the specific criteria developed to include and exclude studies from consideration. These criteria need to be justified in some detail. For example, in reviewing studies comparing men and women on measures of leadership style, Eagly and Johnson (1990) accepted studies only if they had assessed at least five leaders of each sex because extremely small samples would not produce reliable findings. In other reviews, the criteria may limit studies to those that used certain methods (e.g., experiments only), certain populations (e.g., representative samples only), or certain measures. These inclusions and exclusions must make sense in terms of the overall goals of the review.

Exclusions should not appear to be unfair or biased. For example, if the reviewers reject studies using a certain measuring instrument, the problems of that instrument should be documented in some way (by citations of methodological articles).

Reviewers ordinarily proceed to explain how they assembled the meta-analytic database by computing effect sizes and coding the studies. The findings of the meta-analysis emerge from analyses on the effect sizes, especially analyses that relate the coded study attributes to the effect sizes. It is desirable that a referee of a meta-analysis be familiar with how to compute effect sizes under varying conditions (see Lipsey & Wilson, 2001). There are some specialized technical details, for example, concerning the treatment of change scores and dichotomous outcome variables. The referee must therefore scrutinize the description of the effect size calculations to determine whether the reviewers likely proceeded correctly in computing the effect sizes. If the individual effect sizes are not provided in a table in the manuscript, the referee might request access to them by appealing to the editor to obtain this information from the authors. At the very least, the referee should scan these effect sizes for their plausibility.

Referees should pay very close attention to the coding of the studies. The coding should be thorough in terms of assessing basic characteristics (e.g., published versus unpublished source, participant population) as well as many other characteristics that may account for variability in studies' outcomes. Many features of studies' designs, stimuli, and measures could have affected studies' results. Referees should be particularly alert to whether the reviewers have been thorough in assessing quality-relevant features of the studies such as the likely effectiveness of experimental controls and the reliability of the measuring instruments. Other coded attributes should be theory relevant. For example, if competing theories assume differing psychological mediation of the phenomena of interest, then the reviewers should have attempted to assess these mediating processes. If competing theories imply that different variables should moderate the effect of interest, then the reviewers should have assessed these moderators. Good referees thus pay close attention to the list of coded variables; often this scrutiny suggests that quite a few potentially relevant study characteristics were not coded.

Another flaw often detected in the assembling of the meta-analytic database is that no intercoder reliability statistics appear in the manuscript. Apparently only one individual—the author—coded the studies. Single coders are not sufficient even for the coding of study characteristics that require little inference, because the use of two coders makes it possible to catch careless errors. More important, when coding does require inference (e.g., coding studies for how knowledgeable participants were in the domain of the stimulus materials; Eagly, Chen, Chaiken, & Shaw, 1999), considerable training of the coders may be required to produce reliable coding. Evidence of reliable coding generally takes the form of Cohen's kappa or an intraclass correlation (Lipsey & Wilson, 2001). Referees who do not find this evidence in a manuscript should request that the reviewers backtrack to produce this evidence.

Evaluating the Results of a Meta-Analysis

Moving on to the results section of a meta-analysis, referees expect to find two basic components: an overall statistical aggregation of the research findings and analyses accounting for variability in the effect sizes. To produce these findings, reviewers must have carried out appropriate computations. In view of the many technical issues that should affect reviewers' decisions about how to perform these computations, the referee should carefully evaluate whether the reviewers' computational methods are appropriate. Occasionally referees find that the reviewers have used only ordinary descriptive and inferential statistics, not those specifically tailored for meta-analytic data (see Lipsey & Wilson, 2001). In these circumstances, referees call for reanalysis of the effect sizes.

The aggregation presents central tendencies of the effect sizes. Referees should encourage reviewers to present multiple estimates of the central tendencies—for example, in the form of means, medians, and counts of findings' direction in relation to the hypothesis in question. Referees expect the central tendencies to be accompanied by a test of the consistency (or homogeneity) of the effect sizes across the studies. Homogeneous domains of effect sizes are an unusual outcome of a meta-analysis; such an outcome would lead the referee to expect that few, if any, moderators of the effect sizes would appear in the reviewers' subsequent analyses. Ordinarily, if the hypothesis of homogeneity is rejected, the referee expects to find reports of models that successfully accounted for variability in the effect sizes.

Referees should regard accounting for variability in the effect sizes as a mark of success in a meta-analysis. If little variability is accounted for, then the referee should think carefully about whether the coding was well enough designed and executed to capture the study characteristics likely to be correlated with study outcomes. It is not uncommon that the coding of the studies was somewhat minimalist and likely missed important study characteristics. The referee should then recommend that the reviewer return to the coding task to take other variables into account.

Evaluating the Discussion of Meta-Analytic Findings

A reviewer might find the method and results of a meta-analysis to be satisfactory, even exemplary, yet be less than enthusiastic about the project as a whole because the findings do not appear to make much sense in terms of the framework that the reviewer established in the introduction of the manuscript. Excellent reviews yield interesting, interpretable findings. In this respect, review articles are similar to primary research articles, which also must yield interesting, interpretable findings. The referee therefore looks for a summary of the findings that would fix them in readers' minds and then hopes to find an interpretation that encompasses the reported findings and makes good sense in terms of relevant theory. Of course, just as in primary research, the findings may not be in line with expectations based on theory and may therefore lead to some reshaping of theory. Such consequences can be exciting but must be convincingly argued in terms of the findings of the meta-analysis. In general, the conclusions of a meta-analysis must be rigorously connected with its findings. Just as in primary research, empirical findings set the boundaries of the authors' conclusions. Referees have the burden of going back and forth between the results and discussion sections of the review to verify that the authors' claims are true to their findings.

Referee Criteria That Are Relevant Mainly to Narrative Reviews

Some Narrative Reviews Should Be Meta-Analyses

Refereeing narrative reviews is in some senses a more ambiguous, difficult task than refereeing quantitative syntheses. A referee has many specific expectations for a meta-analysis (e.g., thorough searching for studies, thorough coding of studies, intercoder reliability statistics) and notes when the method or analyses are insufficient. Narrative reviews are, in contrast, much freer in their organization and method. They are seldom, if ever, organized in terms of the four classic sections of empirical articles. Therefore, the authors have a greater obligation to thoroughly explain the organization of the manuscript because they cannot rely on any implicit understandings about how such reviews should be structured.

Probably the first question in most contemporary referees' minds is whether a review that has been conducted with narrative methods would better have been conducted as a meta-analysis. If the domain is quite specific within a research literature that produced quantitative findings, then the referee likely will advise the author to return to the drawing board to conduct a meta-analysis. The pitfalls of narrative summaries of groups of research findings are well known (see Johnson & Eagly, 2000). Narrative reviewers all too often interpret research findings in terms of statistical significance. Significance is a poor basis for comparing studies that have different sample sizes, because effects of the same magnitude can differ in statistical significance. Because of this interpretational problem, narrative reviewers may reach erroneous conclusions about a group of studies, even in literatures as small as 10 studies (Cooper & Rosenthal, 1980). Also, narrative reviewers often do not systematically search for relevant studies or state the procedures they used for cataloging the studies' characteristics or evaluating the quality of their methods.

All too often, narrative reviewers do not apply their rules and procedures uniformly to all of the studies in the sample or provide any checks on the reliability of their judgments. Therefore, the review's claims about the characteristics of the studies and the quality of their methods are difficult to evaluate. For example, a manuscript that I recently reviewed, which was a narrative review of a particular domain of social psychology, presented such interpretational problems. The author of the review seemed satisfied with groups of studies that had favored the hypothesis in question, as judged by statistical significance, but seemed dissatisfied with studies that had not favored this hypothesis. The flaws ascribed to the nonconfirming studies were various, but the author presented a plausible reason for each of the nonconfirmations. As a referee, I found it difficult to trust the author's judgment because of the absence of checks on these judgments and the high probability that the rules applied to the nonconfirming studies were not applied uniformly to all of the studies in the sample. It seemed likely that some of the noted flaws had been present in confirming studies as well, but there was no way for me to allay this suspicion by studying the information presented in the manuscript. I thus found the review unconvincing and explained the reasons for my unease in my evaluation of the manuscript.

Many Narrative Reviews Properly Use a Narrative Method

Despite these cautions about narrative reviews that might better have been presented as meta-analyses, the majority of manuscripts that constitute narrative reviews are potentially very valuable contributions to the literature and would not be amenable to quantitative synthesis. Referees should thus realize that in many cases the underlying literature is not quantified in ways that would make meta-analysis feasible and in other cases the breadth of the review precludes meta-analysis. For example, Wood and Eagly (2002) reviewed the ethnographic literature that concerned the male–female division of labor and sex differences in social behavior. Although some of the reviewed studies presented quantitative data, many others were qualitative. Moreover, many of the articles that Wood and Eagly relied on were themselves reviews of anthropologists' studies of diverse cultures. The anthropological reviewers had integrated findings across studies conducted in differing cultures to produce cross-cultural databases to address questions concerning, for example, the extent to which men or women provided a society's basic subsistence. The existence of these large cross-cultural reviews enabled Wood and Eagly to take into account a wide array of ethnographic research. Therefore, refereeing this manuscript was a challenging task that required knowledge of the underlying ethnographic literature and particularly of cross-cultural studies of male and female behavior. Only a knowledgeable referee could evaluate the accuracy of Wood and Eagly's conclusions, because they could not be checked against the presented data in the relatively simple manner in which the conclusions of a meta-analysis can be checked against the presented data.

Sometimes the purpose of a review is the provision of a theoretical framework for organizing a broad area of research. Empirical studies provide illustrations of the usefulness of this framework. In such cases, there may be only a fine line between a theoretical article and a theory-guided narrative review. For example, Kunda and Spencer's (2003) review provided a theoretical framework for understanding the conditions under which stereotypes are activated and applied. Their model hypothesized causal linkages of the psychological processes relevant to applying and suppressing stereotypes. Each of the links was then explicated by citing relevant empirical articles. Some studies were described in detail, and others were merely cited as substantiating certain principles. The authors did not assess the magnitude of any effects or claim that the review was exhaustive of all relevant findings. Rather, Kunda and Spencer presented enough empirical evidence to establish the plausibility of each link in their model. When evaluating this form of review, referees should be sympathetic to the project's purpose and scope but nonetheless somewhat suspicious that the reviewers might have been biased by selecting mainly studies that fit their causal model and ignoring those studies that did not fit it. Only a knowledgeable referee who understands the literature in the research area could judge the fairness of such a review.

Referee's Report

After having studied a review manuscript, a process that generally involves marking up the manuscript with notes, underlining, and question marks, the referee writes his or her evaluative comments for submission to the journal editor. As with all scholarly writing, the referee's report should be well organized and coherent. At this point, it is important for the referee to bring to mind the dual responsibilities of teacher and enforcer of standards. Should the referee's message be unfavorable to the manuscript because it falls substantially below acceptable standards, it is important that the author learns from the evaluation and be convinced that his or her work received a careful analysis. Even when conveying a more favorable evaluation, a referee generally has improvements to suggest in method and statistical analyses in the case of meta-analyses and in presentation and argumentation in the case of review manuscripts of all types. It is essential that suggestions be stated clearly and justified in one way or the other. Especially in the case of meta-analyses, citations of relevant methodological sources or studies exemplifying certain techniques can help guide the author toward a stronger manuscript.

In general, the referee has the burden of documenting her or his claims and criticisms. For example, if the referee maintains that the author has accessed a biased sample of studies, she or he should give examples of the studies that were left out and provide example citations. If the referee believes that the coverage of relevant theories was inadequate, the neglected theories should be named and their relevance explained.

The referee's comments could well start with a tactful statement about the manuscript, if only a sentence or two saying that it tackled an important issue or area. Of course, more detailed praise is in order for strong manuscripts. The referee then would move on to any broad, overarching criticisms of the manuscript—ones that would require that the author rethink the project or backtrack to reanalyze or reassemble the database in the case of meta-analyses.

A referee then generally follows with more specific issues, often organized according to the sections of the manuscript. The form of these specific comments can be a numbered list. The separation of these quite specific comments from broader concerns helps the author sort out the serious problems from the more minor problems, which generally can be easily remedied. This list includes useful advice on writing style if improvement is needed. Length is sometimes a concern of referees as well, because some manuscripts are written in a somewhat leisurely and inefficient style that results in an overly long manuscript. In addition, these listed comments might include praise for especially admirable features of the review.

The referee generally ends with a summary of the strong and the weak aspects of the manuscript and an overall judgment of whether the manuscript is appropriate for the journal to which it was submitted or perhaps appropriate for a different journal. Even if appropriate, the manuscript is typically not ready for publication on its first submission, and the referee may indicate that many or few revisions are needed, consistent with his or her prior comments. These final comments should encourage the author to continue the project, if the project is promising but underdeveloped. Even in the case of badly designed or very poorly developed reviews, which appear to have little potential for publication, the referee should conclude by pointing the way toward a stronger review. With negative judgments, referees need to be especially careful to state their conclusions tactfully.

Additional Rounds of Refereeing

Finally, evaluation criteria differ somewhat when a manuscript is returned to a referee for a second round of evaluation. With literature reviews, two or even three rounds of evaluation are not uncommon because of the complexity of the task of integrating substantial research literatures. In a second round of evaluation, the referee generally has had access to other referees' comments and to the editor's letter to the author. After reading all of the criticisms and comments received by the manuscript, the referee scrutinizes the authors' response to the feedback they received. In general, the authors submit a letter to the editor, which he or she sends on to the referee. The authors may disagree with some referee comments and provide a reasonable justification for their disagreement. Referees expect to find that the authors have either modified their project in line with the advice they received or responded with reasons why they disagree with the advice or find the suggestions impractical. The referees then must carefully read the new manuscript while taking these considerations into account. Most often, review manuscripts are substantially improved when they are submitted a second time. If so, referees can take pride in having helped develop the manuscript. And when a manuscript is published after one or two stages of revision that have been appropriately guided by the refereeing process, all who were involved in mentoring the manuscript ordinarily experience satisfaction that the excellent review is now available to a wider audience.

References

Archer, J. (2000). Sex differences in aggression between heterosexual partners: A meta-analytic review. *Psychological Bulletin, 126,* 651–680.

Bettencourt, B. A., & Miller, N. (1996). Gender differences in aggression as a function of provocation: A meta-analysis. *Psychological Bulletin, 119,* 422–447.

Cooper, H. (2003). Editorial. *Psychological Bulletin, 129,* 3–9.

Cooper, H., & Rosenthal, R. (1980). Statistical versus traditional procedures for summarizing research findings. *Psychological Bulletin, 87,* 442–449.

Eagly, A. H., Chen, S., Chaiken, S., & Shaw, K. (1999). The impact of attitudes on memory: An affair to remember. *Psychological Bulletin, 125,* 64–89.

Eagly, A. H., & Johnson, B. T. (1990). Gender and leadership style: A meta-analysis. *Psychological Bulletin. 108,* 233–256.

Greenwald, A. G. (1975). Consequences of prejudice against the null hypothesis. *Psychological Bulletin, 82,* 1–20.

ISI Journal Citation Reports. (2005). *Psychology.* Retrieved February 8, 2005, from http://isi17.isiknowledge.com.turing.library.northwestern.edu/portal.cgi/jcr/

Johnson, B. T., & Eagly, A. H. (2000). Quantitative synthesis of social psychological research. In H. T. Reis & C. M. Judd (Eds.), *Handbook of research methods in social and personality psychology* (pp. 496–528). New York: Cambridge University Press.

Kunda, A., & Spencer, S. J. (2003). When do stereotypes come to mind and when do they color judgment? A goal-based theoretical framework for stereotype activation and application. *Psychological Bulletin, 129,* 522–544.

Lipsey, M. W., & Wilson, D. B. (2001). *Practical meta-analysis*. Thousand Oaks, CA: Sage.

Wood, W., & Eagly, A. H. (2002). A cross-cultural analysis of the behavior of women and men: Implications for the origins of sex differences. *Psychological Bulletin, 128*, 699–727.

Reviewing Book Proposals

Gary R. VandenBos, Julia Frank-McNeil,
and Judith Amsel

I magine you have been asked by a well-respected publishing house to review a proposal for a scholarly book in psychology. The publisher has selected you, an expert in the field, to assist with the most important decision a publisher makes, deciding whether to develop and publish a specific book being proposed. As a proposal reviewer, you will recommend whether a book proposal represents the current knowledge in the field well, will move the field of psychology forward in some manner, and can be financially successful for the publisher. Your review weighs heavily in the publishing decision that the publisher will make. You take this request seriously. You are pleased to be considered an expert and curious about a view into the publishing world. You might also be a little intimidated by the fact that you are being asked to review the proposal of a prominent and senior scholar in your field. You want to do a professional job for the publisher by providing a valuable and credible review. But you also wonder how reviewing for a book publisher is different from reviewing journal articles. To understand this, you need a little background on scholarly book publishing.

Overview of Book Publishing in Psychology

Psychology publishing houses vary in size, style, and purpose. Some larger houses publish all types of scholarly books— reference works, textbooks, scholarly and professional books, and popular (trade) titles. However, many publishers focus on a more limited range of book types. Commercial (or for-profit) publishers operate side-by-side with university presses and the publishing arms of nonprofit organizations, such as the American Psychological Association. The publishing mission of these different types of publishers can vary. Books are sold in hardcover (cloth), soft cover (paperback), and electronic format to buyers who may be researchers, college students, practitioners, or educated laypeople. And, the books published may be singly or multiply authored books, edited collections, or compilations of previously published works.

Any given publisher has a mission or target audience or content specialty. It may be to provide quality educational textbooks for undergraduates, educate the general public on specific psychological topics, disseminate the highest quality and most cutting-edge scientific research, provide outstanding reference products for the given academic field, inform policymakers about research related to emerging social issues, or provide busy practitioners with the latest information on new clinical techniques. Thus, a publisher decides to offer a book contract for a specific book for a host of reasons related to the particular audience that they are trying to reach.

However, book publishing, whether by a commercial publisher or a not-for-profit publisher, is a business. A book publishing program needs to make a profit (or at least minimize loss). Thus, a key element of what a publisher needs to assess is the potential market for a given book, its revenue potential, and the financial risk (and how to minimize that financial risk). It is the consideration of these factors that makes book proposal evaluation somewhat different from evaluating a journal article.

One step all publishers have in common is that they need the assistance of experts in the course of evaluating proposals and manuscripts. Acquiring editors usually do not have an in-depth knowledge of each psychological specialty area in which their press publishes. Proposals need to be vetted and reviewed by content experts. The editor must rely on the opinions of those who have a thorough knowledge of the literature of each sub-specialty of the field.

The overarching purpose of the review of a book proposal is to explore the likelihood that the manuscript will provide the value, in terms of content and marketability, the publisher hopes to deliver. The proposal reviewer is evaluating, in essence, how well the proposed configuration of the outlined book will fit the stated vision or mission of the work (and the relationship it will have to the intended audience of potential users and purchasers). To assist in this, the reviewer needs to have some understanding of the audience that the author and the publisher are intending to reach, as well as the market potential of the proposed work.

Before You Begin . . .

You need to know what is expected from you by the publisher and in what form the publisher expects your feedback. There are at least three things you should consider before you agree to evaluate a book proposal.

1. Make certain that you have a clear understanding of exactly what the publisher wants in the review. If you are in doubt, ask the publisher or the publisher's representative. Clarify up front the purpose of the review. You want to know if the publisher wants an intelligent opinion on the general worth of the project, a mid-level analysis of the overall organization and major topics areas, a detailed and careful page-by-page analysis for manuscript shaping and development, or something else.
2. Make certain that you are an appropriate individual to review the given proposal. Do you, in fact, have the relevant expertise? If you are not the right person to review the proposal, tell the publisher—and tell the publisher immediately. You might wish to recommend others who you believe have more directly

relevant expertise for evaluating the book proposal. Doing this will get you remembered in a positive light as someone who was honest and helpful.

3. Make certain that you have the time to review the book proposal within the time frame that the publisher is seeking. If you do not have the time, then let the publisher know right away. Publishing is a competitive business. A timely response to a proposal is critical to both the publisher and the author. Nothing is worse than waiting 3 to 4 weeks for a review, only to find out that the reviewer has declined the offer to review the proposal. Remember, you are developing a reputation that goes with your name.

What Does a Book Proposal Look Like?

Book proposals vary in format. Some are little more than a brief outline of the proposed volume or a table of contents. Others have detailed descriptions of each chapter, and in some cases, sample chapters or even a complete draft of the manuscript are sent with the proposal.

The standard proposal format for an authored book that most publishers request includes a synopsis of the proposed book, stating its mission, purpose, and goal; an annotated table of contents; some type of chapter outline or statement of what specifically will be in each chapter; proposed manuscript length and delivery date; a description of market potential, including competitive works; and biographical information on the authors or editors. A sample chapter can also be helpful, but is usually not essential.

What Does the Publisher Want?

Typically the reviewer is provided with a list of questions from the publisher to help frame the reviewer's evaluation of the proposal. These questions are crafted to help orient you in your evaluation of the proposal. The publisher may have a slightly different set of questions for different types of book (edited, authored, professional, text, or trade), but the questions are usually general questions that are not specific to the given book. You will need to do more than just answer the stated questions to be of maximum assistance to the publisher. Nonetheless, the basic questions all publishers ask are fundamentally the same:

- ☐ Does the plan for the proposed volume appear sound? Is it a balanced plan?
- ☐ Is the projected content comprehensive, appropriate, and timely?
- ☐ Are the suggested chapters appropriately focused? Should any chapters be added or deleted?
- ☐ Do the chapters provide strong theoretical and empirical support?
- ☐ What do you think of the orientation of this volume? Does it represent current scientific and professional knowledge in a balanced way?
- ☐ Do you believe that there is a need as well as a market for the proposed book?

Questions to consider in developing your assessment of a book proposal include the following:

Questions About the Author. Exactly who is the proposing author or authors or editor? Has the author written about the proposed topic of the book in earlier journal articles or book chapters? Is the author known and respected in the subspecialty of the proposed volume? If the author is a relatively new scholar in the field or subspecialty, what evidence is there that he or she knows enough about the area to write an entire book on the topic? Is this the best author to write this proposed work, or at least a reasonable candidate to write the proposed book? If the proposed volume is an edited book, is the editor proposing the best chapter authors (or at least ones who are qualified to write the chapters)? The appropriate match of proposed chapter authors to specific chapter topics will provide you with information on how well the editor knows who is active in the specialty area and the particular topics within the area.

You will also want to think about the known biases of the author. Is the author in any known camps within the specialty area, and how open to and accepting of the views from the other camps is the author? You, too, will need to put aside your biases to provide publishers with professional information to help them make their decisions. If you cannot do this, then inform the publisher and decline the opportunity to review the proposal.

Finally, you must consider whether the author can deliver the proposed manuscript in terms of high-quality, well-written content and by the expected deadline. What do you know of the author's reputation in terms of the quality of the first submitted drafts and in terms of meeting the professional commitments in a timely manner? It does the publisher no good to sign contracts for books that will never be delivered or book manuscripts that will take long (and expensive) hours to clean up and get to a publishable level.

Questions About the Content Area. The publisher uses the review process to test the quality of the theoretical, empirical, and practical information described in the proposal. At a minimum, every manuscript must be factually accurate, state fairly and clearly expository generalizations, use cited references from the high-quality peer-reviewed published material, and provide insight and understanding. The review of the book proposal provides the primary method of scientific quality control in book publishing.

In your review you will address questions such as the following: Is the material accurate? Is the information up-to-date and current? Are the needed basic terms defined, and defined correctly? Is the relevant literature needed as background adequately reviewed and described? Is the author proposing the right mix of content? Is the organization and order of the material and chapters the most useful one? Does the argument the author presents follow a logical progression? Is the topic of the proposed book in a burgeoning area or in a specialty area for which there is already a considerable body of published material? Does the field need this book, and why?

Is the topic of the proposed volume a controversial topic? Will this proposed book add to the discussion? If this is a controversial topic, then the information should be given about the controversy, the possibility of disagreement, and the best approach for a balanced presentation. Some publishers seek controversial books, and others avoid them. Controversial books often sell well if they are well prepared and do not ignore issues or make claims that cannot be supported by available evidence. Sometimes with a controversial book, the publisher will seek proposal reviews from scholars who are known to support an opposing theory or approach to the one being explored in the proposed work. The publisher may want to see the criticism of the ideas and data to be included in the proposed book in advance of contracting or publishing.

However detailed the presentation of the proposed book, the reviewer must respond to the information that is presented and not guess the author's intention. If you have to make assumptions about what the author will cover or what the logical argument will be, it may mean that the author has not been concrete and specific enough in the proposal. The reviewer should tell the publisher if the materials are too scant to evaluate with confidence. If the reviewer wants additional information before making a recommendation, the publisher may be able to obtain more information from the author of the proposed book.

Questions About the Audience and Market. The publisher wants to know where the proposed new book fits into the array of book material that already exists. As an expert in the area, the publisher is counting on you to provide this information. The publisher assumes you have read the potentially competing works in the field, and that you know what topics have not been covered or adequately covered in book form. Is this proposed work similar to what already exists, or is it different? What are the other competing titles? Will similarity in scope and content be a marketing plus, or will the proposed volume be viewed as just another in a long line of books covering the same old tired material? If there are a number of similar books already in the market of the proposed topic, then does the proposed book have an approach that will allow it to penetrate the existing market and capture a share of it? Or, alternatively, will the proposed volume be the first book-length treatment of a topic? Is the field ready for this book? Is there adequate research to support the volume? Is there a theory or framework around which a volume can be built? Is this author the one that readers would expect to be the author of the first book in this emerging area? If not, is this author a credible candidate to author the first book on this topic?

To what primary and secondary audience will this book appeal? The question is not whether a given audience would benefit from reading the proposed volume. Rather, the question is whether the book will have enough appeal to get those in a given audience to purchase the volume and read it. How big do you believe the audience for this book might be? Is the book so broad and central to the field that realistically the potential audience is all licensed mental health professionals, or is it very narrow and only of interest to those in the overlap area between two subspecialties? A book on the assessment and treatment of depression would be relevant to a very large proportion of licensed mental health professionals, whereas a volume on the psychology of female serial murderers would have a much more limited audience, as the average licensed mental health professional will never encounter or treat such a patient.

Writing the Review Report for the Publisher

Write your review of the book proposal in a collegial and collaborative manner. Reviewers who make personal characterizations or slant their critique to wound instead of enlighten are posturing, not collaborating. Although one purpose of having you evaluate a book proposal is to assess its quality, the market for it, and the potential financial success of it, another purpose of getting your evaluation is to improve and enhance the content and organization of the book (so it will have broader appeal and will sell more copies) and make an overall advancement of the field. Thus, evaluating a book proposal needs to be a collaborative process that improves the book and advances the field. Sometimes you will be asked to evaluate a proposal from one of your favorite scholars. In those cases, avoid excessive or inappropriate praise. Critical or supercilious reviews do not serve the field or the publisher.

The book proposal review report that you write will vary in length, depending on what you have to say and the needs of the publisher, but an average-length report might be a two-to-three-page document. Such a document might take about 2 hours to write, after you have read the proposal and consider any information provided with the proposal. Your review is not a literary document or one that will be published. Instead, the review is a clear, concise, straightforward evaluation of the proposed book that meets the publisher's needs for evaluating the strength of the content in the proposed volume for purposes of making a decision about whether to offer a contract to the author to publish the book.

Provide editorial feedback, but do not lapse into technical editing of the proposal by correcting typos and grammatical errors in the proposal or draft chapters. The publisher has technical editors to do that. You are being asked to comment on content and the organization of content.

Reviews may go beyond the specific questions from the publisher. Books generally develop linear arguments. Tell the publisher whether this one does, whether it is effective, and what, if anything, needs to be done to improve this aspect of the proposed volume. Sometimes, a manuscript may be enhanced by devices such as information placed in lists, boxed information to present specific content, case studies, graphics and illustrations, and appended information. Are there other creative features that could be added to the volume (e.g., work sheets, forms, figures, or tables) that would improve effective communication or usability of information? If you have an idea for an alternative means of presenting or understanding the material (or another technique of rhetoric), suggest ways in which to improve the structure of the proposed book or otherwise present the information more effectively.

It is important to think about the array of potential readers of your review report (e.g., acquiring editor, author, production editor, and media relations specialist) because you want to write in a style that all will understand. Some publishing programs share reviewers' comments verbatim with authors, other reviewers, and internal staff. Some publishers allow limited access to specific review commentary, but they may paraphrase it in letters to authors, editors, and others. Provide an honest assessment of the proposed book. Tell the publisher exactly what you think about the material. Do not mince words, but do not grandstand. This is not an opportunity for you to promote your own position (or to undercut someone else's). Rather, it is your job to provide a thoughtful critique of the material in terms of the value this product will yield to the publisher (and the field).

As you are reading the book proposal and writing your evaluative report, remember that you have been hired by the publisher as a content expert to assist in their vital publishing decision-making efforts. Your task is to respond to all aspects of the proposed book's content and success in communicating. Be thorough, thoughtful, and decisive.

What's in It for You?

First, the publisher will pay you. Not a lot, and the hourly rate will not turn out to be high, but the publisher will pay you for your time. Alternatively, many publishers are reimbursing reviewers in the form of credits toward books published by the publisher. Second, you can list "editorial consultant" for the publisher on your vita as an additional example of your expertise and professional activities. Third, your efforts will benefit the field by improving the quality of the books published for and in the field. Fourth, it represents another part of your professional responsibility for advancing the field. Fifth, you are providing a professional courtesy by assisting colleagues in improving their contribution and efforts. And, finally, you will learn about book publishing—and that will probably help you in your own career advancement. As a book proposal reviewer, you become an insider in the publisher's scholarly and business process. Someday you may be writing a book, and your experience as a reviewer will give you an insider's view of publishing, such as what a publisher wants, how to prepare a book proposal, and how to assess what might be a new hot topic on which to write. Moreover, you may become a friend to the press, and they may eventually solicit a book proposal from you.

6

Reviewing Book Chapters

Henry L. Roediger III

R eviewing chapters that will appear in books is quite different from reviewing standard journal articles. This fact is partly because book chapters are invited contributions, partly because of the type of people who are invited to write chapters, partly because chapters rarely have the detail and complexity of journal articles, and partly because of the lighter demands of the job itself. The assumption in reviewing a book chapter is that the chapter will probably be published; the job of the reviewer is primarily to make suggestions for improvement. Conversely, the assumption in reviewing an article for most of psychology's selective journals is that the article has a high probability of rejection, certainly on first submission. Therefore the reviewer's approach and mind-set are quite different in the two cases.

This chapter first describes the process by which an edited volume goes from the idea in the editor's mind to the reality of a book several years later, because this information is critical for knowing how to review a chapter. The remainder of the chapter involves tips on reviewing the chapter itself.

The Edited Volume

The bookshelves of all psychologists are filled with edited volumes. These kinds of contributions were fairly rare (for whatever reason) until around 1970. At one point, edited volumes often achieved great importance in the field. In "experimental psychology," as the fields of basic animal and human psychology were called in the 1950s, S. S. Stevens's *Handbook of Experimental Psychology* (1951) was the bible of the field and guided generations of students. Today it is rare to find an edited volume that everyone in even a subfield of psychology must buy and know because of the glut of such books on the market. Still, occasionally a must-have edited volume is published. In my field, *The Oxford Handbook of Memory* has achieved this status (Tulving & Craik, 2000), but few other edited books have in recent years.

Why are there so many edited volumes? The reasons are numerous, but one is economic. Book publishers discovered that if they published an edited volume, some 500 to 1,000 libraries at research universities would buy them. If the book were priced high enough, a tidy profit could be made. If the book were also bought by individuals and perhaps even used in graduate seminars, then so much the better.

The idea of an edited volume may come from the publisher or from the academic editors. For example, the editor at the publishing company might discover a niche that he or she believes needs to be filled. A light goes off in the editor's head one day and he or she thinks, "There is no *Handbook of Armadillo Psychology*." Even if there is no real need or demand for this handbook, some libraries will buy it (they seem to buy any authoritative reference work). So the publisher will go out and try to find a leading expert on armadillo psychology to develop the handbook. This researcher, your typical ambitious academic, jumps at the chance to edit the authoritative handbook in his or her field. Of course, the publisher offers little money to the editor and provides a contract specifying the duties of the editor, as discussed below.

The impetus for the book in this scenario comes from the publishing company, but probably most edited volumes are created in the reverse manner. That is, an academic expert on some topic decides he or she wants to edit a book on a particular topic. The expert writes a prospectus for the book explaining its rationale and perhaps providing a tentative list of chapters and a wish list of authors to write those chapters. Sometimes the editor even tries to get commitments from the prospective authors that they will indeed write the chapters if the book is approved by a publishing company.

Assuming that a contract is signed, it specifies the duties of the editor. The list is long and would include the following steps to be carried out over the period of months and years: finding authors, cajoling them into writing for the handbook, providing them a template for the chapter (so the chapters will be of roughly the same organization and style), setting deadlines for delivery of the chapters, and sending reminders to authors to nag them to get their chapters in near the deadline. After the chapters have finally arrived, the editor sends them out for review (that is where you come in as a reviewer). Reviewers might be offered a small honorarium but often are simply asked to review the chapters with only the promise of receiving a free copy of the book. The editor then goes into nagging mode with the reviewers (perhaps there are two reviewers for each chapter, and often they are other authors of the book). When the reviews are in for each chapter, the editor must read the chapter along with the reviews and write a letter to the author providing advice. In very rare cases, the chapter might be rejected as unworthy of inclusion (even leading experts can ignore writing the chapter or pass it along to a graduate student who is not up to the task). More likely, the editor writes each author a letter providing suggestions based on the reviews and on the editor's own expert opinion. Because chapters come in and are reviewed at an uneven pace, the editor's process of reviewing the chapters may extend over many months, depending on the editor's efficiency in cracking the whip to get contributions in and get responses from authors.

Let us consider some of the stages in more detail. The process is a long one, but as noted, the first step is for the editor to write a flattering letter to the 25 (or so) prospective authors saying that the world's first authoritative handbook on armadillo psychology (or whatever) is being created and each is being invited to write about his or her specialty for the handbook. Their reward will be a free copy of the book and (maybe) $100. Of course, the real reason the author is writing is for that more elusive quality of fame (i.e., "Everyone will know that I am one of the leading armadillo psychologists in the world, and I get to tell my version of the truth about my topic of study"). Publishers love academics because they will do a tremendous amount of hard work and not expect to get paid for it. The book publishers get paid for the academics' work.

Once the 25 authors are lined up, the editor's job is to provide the authors with a structure for their chapters so the final book will not have chapters organized in 25 different ways. Of course, even with the editor providing guidelines, some academics are notoriously obstinate about not following them, with each having his or her own idea about how to do the job better than the editor. Still, with luck, the chapters should look more or less the same. The editor sets a due date for the first draft of the chapters, perhaps 6 to 12 months after the instructions are given for writing the chapter. Most authors begin either as the due date approaches or, more probably, just after the due date has passed. The editor's main job at this point is to constantly nag the authors to make them feel guilty, get the chapter in, and get the editor off his or her back.

Once the editor gets the first draft of the chapters in hand, that is where you (as the reviewer) come into play. The chapters are usually sent to one or two reviewers for comment. You may be a young, up-and-coming armadillo psychologist, so you are flattered at being asked for your opinion of a chapter by the acknowledged leader in your area. Being an academic, you do not think of asking the publisher for money for your review. Instead, you will work for many hours for the honor of commenting on the chapter (and maybe $50 or some free books from the publisher). But, importantly, you also get to learn about what a leading expert thinks about your field a couple of years before most of the world has the chance to see the chapter. The nature of your review will be discussed in the next section.

Once you have sent your review in, the editor of the volume will combine his or her thoughts with yours and (possibly) another reviewer's and will write an action letter to the author of the chapter. The author will then be asked to revise and resubmit the chapter. Once this process has occurred for all 25 chapters, the editor will perform other chores (writing a preface, for example) and transmit the whole manuscript to the publisher. The publisher may then seek some outside reviews on the whole project: Is this handbook good? Should the company publish it or pull the plug on it? (This is always the company's right, as specified in contracts, but of course the publisher is hoping for good reviews because they have already devoted time, cost, and effort to the project.) The publisher may ask the book's editor and authors for additional revisions at this point. Eventually the editor at the publishing company will probably decide that the manuscript is good enough and begin the production process. This is a long process carried out at the company. The manuscript must be copyedited and then approved by the author. Then the author will receive at least one stage and possibly two stages of proofing the printed manuscript. All changes must be made by the final proofing stage. The final task that remains is to prepare a subject index or an author index. Depending on the terms of the contract, these are either the responsibility of the company or the author. Finally, 2 to 3 years (or more) after the entire process began, the final product should emerge and you will receive your copy of the *Handbook of Armadillo Psychology, First Edition.*

Reviewing the Chapter

For the reasons cited previously, reviewing chapters is much easier in most ways than reviewing articles. Because the authors are invited, they have usually established themselves as experts. The editor has already selected the authors to write the chapters, and the editor hopes to publish them (unless they are dreadful). Therefore, your job as the reviewer is much different than in journal reviewing. In addition, chapters are usually (but not always) summaries of research and conclusions, written at a relatively general level. The complicated analyses on which general conclusions are based are usually provided in the primary journal articles. Your job as reviewer is to ask and answer some fundamental questions that apply to all chapters.

Is the Chapter Wrong for the Book? Is It Bad?

Did the author understand the purpose and do a good job in fulfilling it? The answers are usually yes, but you must consider these questions. Most invited authors are very good researchers, but they are often overcommitted. When it comes time to write the chapter, they might simply not put the thought and care into it that the chapter deserves. One scenario is that as the deadline approached, the author might simply have dashed something off and sent it in. Or the author might have decided to hand off the chapter to a graduate student or colleague and become second author. Now the chapter is not really what the editor commissioned—an authoritative chapter by a leading expert in the field. In fact, some editors specify that the invited author must be first author on the chapter to avoid this problem of diffusion of responsibility.

If the chapter is simply substandard and is by a senior figure in the field, there is nothing else to do but say this in a direct manner (but as gently as possible). I once saw a masterful letter to an author saying, in effect, that "I really want to publish a chapter by you in this book, but if we publish the one you submitted, we will both be greatly embarrassed when the book comes out." So the editor seemed to be looking out for the author by protecting the author's reputation. To his credit, on reflection the author agreed in this case. The final chapter was much improved.

So, if the chapter is bad, the reviewer must simply advise the editor that the chapter should not be published in anything like its current form. The chapter's author should thank you (although of course your review is probably anonymous) for avoiding embarrassment, as in the above example. However, that might be asking too much of most authors. At this point in the process, the editor can give the author another chance and ask for a thorough revision. Indeed, this is the most probable scenario because the editor has asked the author to write and it is embarrassing to reject a chapter by a top person in the field writing on the topic he or she is supposed to know best. (Rejecting the chapter will surely alienate the author, who may retaliate in some way at some later point.) So, chances are that even a bad first draft will be eventually published, although it may take a couple of rounds of revision to make it publishable. To be honest, it may be published even if the reviewers and editor doubt that it should be.

What Steps Can Be Taken to Produce a Better Chapter?

Happily, this question is usually the one that faces the reviewer. The chapter is fair to good (or maybe even excellent), but your job as reviewer is to provide suggestions to make it even better. This can be done by answering questions to sharpen the chapter.

Is the Writing Consistently Clear? Chapters are sometimes written by two or three authors, each of whom is responsible for various sections of the chapter. The authors will have different styles and cover different topics. The lead author should take the responsibility for striving to revise the chapter and make it a seamless whole. However, this sometimes does not occur and the reviewers should point to spots where the writing is murky, the logic unclear, or where the points in the chapter seem inconsistent (or, more likely, repetitive, as different authors cover the same topic or study). Even when a single author writes the chapter, he or she can be myopic, spilling into technical terms and seeming to assume that the reader has put down the author's latest papers before picking up the chapter. The reviewer should point out places where the author assumes too much background knowledge on the part of the reader. In general, it is a good idea for authors to define technical terms briefly and to avoid the use of initials to stand for conditions or terms. The reviewer should insist that the author write clearly and explain terms to the interested nonspecialist.

Is the Literature Fairly Reviewed? Are critical studies bearing on the points in the chapter omitted or given short shrift? The mission of the author writing a chapter can vary. The editor should tell you in a cover letter asking you to review the chapter what task the author undertook. If the chapter you are reviewing is for a handbook or other reference book, then the author's task is to dispassionately review the literature and to be relatively inclusive of the critical aspects of the literature on that topic. Of course, authors will differ on what to include and how to treat various topics; some variability among experts in how to treat a topic is to be expected. Still, the reviewer's task is to make certain the author's license to define the literature on a topic does not go too far. Has the author covered the major topics in the field under review? Are some topics given too much space relative to others? Have other topics been completely omitted or given too little attention? Are critical bodies of evidence that would change conclusions in the chapter ignored? The reviewer should ask these questions while reading the chapter.

Many edited volumes do not ask for a dispassionate review of the field on some topic. Rather, the purpose of the volume is to let each of the authors provide his or her perspective on the issue. Therefore, unlike handbooks or encyclopedias, many edited volumes permit the author to define what she or he will write about. If the nature of the chapter is to put forward the author's point of view or to review the author's program of research on a particular topic, then the reviewer of the chapter need not worry so much about inclusiveness of topics and so forth. Still, however, the reviewer should consider literature that has been omitted and that might change the author's story.

One pleasure in writing a chapter for an edited volume is that the author is usually given great latitude in what he or she writes without having to satisfy nitpicking reviewers and editors. Although a comfort, some authors can take the practice too far and write only about their own work to the exclusion of relevant literature, precursors of their ideas, or even research that directly contradicts the authors' conclusions. The reviewer's task in these cases is at least to point out these omissions and to warn the author when a tendency toward perceived bias is too great. These comments can be made as take-it-or-leave-it suggestions ("here is my reaction to your chapter . . . ") and then the author (and editor) can decide what to do about your comments. So, give it your best shot in a gentle way to improving coverage, but in the final analysis it is the author's chapter and the author's point of view, not yours or the editor's.

Are Tables and Figures Appropriate? Chapters differ wildly on the inclusion of figures and tables. Some chapters (like this one) are narrative in nature and do not have tables or figures. However, for chapters in which a body of literature is reviewed, tables and figures can be very useful. Chapters often review literature, and sometimes authors can find a clever way of encapsulating data in a figure or table and make a point that does not exist in the literature. Figures and tables also help break up text and can present a visual image of salient data. As a reviewer, you should suggest places where figures or tables could be helpful to the author's argument. In rare cases, when the author has simply recycled too many old tables and figures from journal articles, the reviewer's task is to suggest ways that these can be combined, consolidated, or simply eliminated. Although judicious use of tables and figures can be quite helpful, they do take considerable space, and their overuse can make the text choppy and hard to follow. If tables and figures are made to do too much of the work in communicating the message, then the author might be leaving the reader with too much work to figure it out. The tables and figures should add to, and not replace, careful expository writing.

Is the Chapter an Appropriate Length? The editor has probably set guidelines for length of the chapter. Although it is primarily the editor's responsibility to enforce these guidelines, the reviewers can also comment. In particular, the usual strategy is to give all authors the same length guideline (perhaps 25 pages of double-spaced text, or give them a word count or character count as a target). However, not all topics are deserving of equal space. If the author has gone over the guideline by a sizeable margin, you can comment on whether the chapter is padded and should be cut back to size. Conversely, you can side with the author and argue that the chapter deserves to be published much as the author has written it and that cutting the chapter to fit some arbitrary guideline would gut it and make it worse.

Are There Other Points That Might Strengthen the Author's Arguments? Just as the reviewer might see examples in which authors have overstated their cases, so might the reviewer see places where the author can make his or her case stronger. The reviewer can see how the argument made by the author will extend logically into another realm, or the reviewer might know of an experiment that would bolster the author's case.

One danger in helpfully extending the author's case is to be too generous. That is, suppose a really good idea occurs to you during the review process. Do you give it to the author, who can then appropriate it for his or her own? Or do you save it for yourself for some future publication? And, if you decide the latter, is it unethical to hold the idea back? These issues are judgment calls. A rough guideline might be that if your idea is really directly related to what the author is writing or if you would be unlikely to ever pursue a parallel line of work, make the point in your review. Human nature being what it is, what you perceive as wonderful, fresh insight might not be appreciated by the author, anyway. However, if your work is related to the author's work (and there is a high probability of this being the case, which is why you were asked to review the chapter), and if you suddenly have a blinding insight while reading the chapter that you might convert into an interesting series of studies that would provide critical insights to the issues at hand, you are under no obligation to design these experiments for the author to pursue. If you so choose, you could use the author's ideas (appropriately credited, of course) as a springboard for your own series of experiments. Gaining ideas from chapters you are reviewing in this way is no different from having ideas about chapters that are already published. Part of the recompense in reviewing chapters is to give you a chance to think hard about problems in which you are interested and to read the perspective of a leader in the field a year or two before the reading public will get to see the chapter. Indeed, often your ideas derived from reading the chapter will be the only compensation for your review.

What Is Good About the Chapter? Reviewing, by its nature, tends to be a highly critical process. The reviewer's job, in part, is to find fault. Some reviewers tend to think this is their only job, but good reviewers know better: Their job is to evaluate the chapter or manuscript at hand and point out good and bad features. I try to begin and end my reviews with positive comments and would urge others to do the same. Do not be afraid to say what is good about the chapter. If done at the end, one can adopt the tone (when appropriate) that "Although my review has raised a number of critical points, my overall appraisal of this chapter is that it should be published. Attention to my comments would, in my opinion, make a good chapter even better." Of course, you cannot say something this positive for every chapter or paper you review, but try to get across *some* positive information to the author if at all possible, someplace in the review. As you know from being on the receiving end of reviews, there is nothing more depressing than reading a long litany of nitpicking criticisms for a chapter or paper that you, the author, spent so much time on and believe is so good. If you as a reviewer cannot find positive comments to say about the chapter (or paper) you are reviewing, this fact may reflect as much or more about you than it does about the chapter and author being reviewed.

Conclusion

Reviewing chapters can give the reviewer new insights and let him or her see what may be an important book 2 years or more before it is published. The questions posed in this chapter are a good starting place for reviewing a chapter. Great reviewers, ones who can look at the big picture and convey constructive criticism, are among the unsung heroes of academia. Although many people complain about the reviewing process (and some features of the process are, or at least can be, harmful), I believe the overall product of the peer review system is a very good one, in the long run (Roediger, 1987). To paraphrase Winston Churchill's remark about democracy, peer review may not be the best system to decide what scientific material to publish, but it is better than all the others that have been tried.

References

Roediger, H. L. (1987). The role of journal editors in the scientific process. In D. N. Jackson & J. P. Rushton (Eds.), *Scientific excellence: Origins and assessment* (pp. 222–252). New York: Sage.

Stevens, S. S. (Ed.). (1951). *Handbook of experimental psychology.* New York: Wiley.

Tulving, E., & Craik, F. I. M. (2000). *The Oxford handbook of memory.* Oxford, England: Oxford University Press.

Chapter 7

Reviewing Grant and Contract Proposals

Paul A. Gade, David P. Costanza,
and Jonathan D. Kaplan

A s Norman (1986) has clearly pointed out, the peer review process has an impact on the science of psychology in two very important ways. First, the process is the primary determinant in the dissemination of research results in peer-reviewed publications. Second, and probably even more important, the peer-review process has a major impact on the allocation of grant and contract funds to behavioral scientists to do their research. The funding decisions determine to a great extent what research does or does not get done.

Given the importance of the peer reviewing process for grants and contracts, we were surprised to find that most studies of and articles giving advice about the peer review process have focused on reviewing articles for publication (e.g., Drotar, 2000; Epstein, 1995; Hadjistavropoulos & Bierling, 2000) or how to write a grant/contract proposal (e.g., Coley & Scheinberg, 2000;

The views, opinions, and findings contained in this article are solely those of the authors and should not be construed as an official Department of the Army or Department of Defense position, policy, or decision, unless so designated by other documentation.

Stamper, 1995; Sternberg, 2004). Perhaps this is because the peer review processes for grant and contract proposals developed independently of the peer review process for scientific publication (Hemlin, 1999). Fortunately, the broad factors that make for a good review of a journal article, book, book chapter, or grant/contract proposal are the same: In all cases, reviews that are unbiased, competent, constructive, and free from ad hominem personal attacks are the objective. These broad factors are not orthogonal and, as a result, overlap to some degree, as we shall see.

Peer reviews by appropriate professionals, be they for publication or funding grant/contract proposals, require the highest levels of professional competence and ethics on the part of all those involved in the review process. Although professional competence is usually well accounted for in the grant proposal review process, ethical issues concerning bias and, especially, personal attacks are often ignored or swept under the rug. Thus, it is important to deal first with the broad issues of competency, bias, and personal attacks generally and then more specifically as they apply to the various steps of the grant/contract proposal peer review process.

Competency in the Review Process

Professional competency in the peer review process refers to the requirement that those who do the peer reviews be knowledgeable professionals in the area or areas of research being reviewed and therefore qualified to make professional judgments about the quality of the research proposed. Professional ethical principles demand that those who seek reviewers for proposals select and invite only those they know to be competent in the research area being reviewed. In turn, these principles also demand that researchers asked to perform peer reviews decline such invitations if they do not feel they are competent to perform such reviews. This may not always be as easy as it seems, because it is usually a high compliment to be asked to be a reviewer and, in some cases, reviewers may be paid well for their services. Given the importance of the reviewing process on funding decisions, the issue of reviewer competency should not be underestimated.

Drotar (2000) suggested that the essence of any competent peer review is thoroughness, clarity and specificity, constructiveness, tact, and timeliness. Thoroughness means that the reviewer, after carefully reading the proposal, provides detailed, point-by-point evaluative comments for each major section of the proposal. In some cases this may require line-by-line feedback. Clarity demands specificity. Merely stating that the data collection plan was problematic, for example, is insufficient. Detailed, precise feedback regarding strengths, yes strengths, as well as weaknesses is what is required. Even if the feedback is clear and detailed, reviewers need to provide constructive suggestions for improving the proposal. These will be useful to the author in preparing future proposals and may be useful to the author and the agency in strengthening proposals selected for funding. Tact in delivering negative feedback should be a goal for every reviewer and a matter of ethical, professional behavior. Even more so than publication reviews, timeliness is critical for completing proposal reviews. The proposal review process tends to be longer and involve more people and group decisions than do publication reviews; therefore, it is even more critical to the process that reviews be completed on time.

Reviewer Biases

Reviewers need to be aware of and guard against the biases that seem to be inherent in the review process and that may be operating in the review situation in which they find themselves. Some of the biases we know about in the grant/contract review process are common to the peer review process in general, whereas some are unique to grant/contract proposal reviewing. In general, reviewers of manuscripts submitted for publication and proposed grants/contracts tend to be too positive or lenient in their reviews (Hemlin, 1999; Norman, 1986). This seems to be particularly true when the guidance for the review is broad and vague—usually this is a greater problem for publication reviews than for grant/contract proposal reviews. This bias also seems to be somewhat less prevalent among more experienced reviewers, which is one of many good reasons for teaching students to be reviewers as well as authors (Jayasinghe, Marsh, & Bond, 2003).

In the absence of clear guidance in the review process, the idiosyncratic subjective values of grant proposal reviewers operate freely. Norman (1986) showed that peer reviewers with little external guidance tend to have a strong bias toward accepting proposals. He also showed that such reviewers tend to rely most heavily on information from the text of the proposal and information about the researcher who authored the proposal. Furthermore, in the absence of clear guidance, reviewers tend to strengthen their views when they are exposed to similar views from other reviewers but are largely unaffected by opposing views. The grant/contract proposal review process may be particularly prone to this sort of bias when reviewers are brought together, in real time or virtually, to resolve multiple reviews of the same proposal. This may result in less differentiation among proposals and hence make the final funding decisions much more difficult. As we have seen, peer reviewers tend to be biased toward giving positive overall judgments to the articles or proposals they review; however, they also tend to accentuate the negative aspects of these same articles and proposals in the comments that they provide in their reviews at the expense of providing more constructive criticism. For example, in a study of peer-reviewed articles for the *Journal of Applied Behavior Analysis*, Boice, Pecker, Zaback, and Barlow (1985) found that peer reviewers were far more "generous" with negative comments than with constructive criticisms and more condescending with rejected articles than with those that were accepted. Other researchers of the peer review process have pointed out that reviewers often find it easier to accentuate the faults of a proposal while failing to offer constructive criticism (Drotar, 2000).

In some cases the negative effects were so pronounced in the grant/contract review process that funding agencies have been forced to adopt specific practices intended to minimize their impact. The National Science Foundation (NSF), for example, has a special procedure for dealing with accusations of impropriety, fraud, or unethical behavior made by its reviewers (J. Young, personal communication, October, 2003). Other agencies require reviewers to read and sign disclosure forms covering conflicts of interest, ethics policies, and reviewing guidelines. These pre-emptive actions suggest that granting agencies may need to pay particular attention to such biases before making funding decisions.

Another area of potential bias is the implicit connections made by many reviewers between the people doing the research and the research itself. For example, in examining the Australian Research Council's large grant program, Marsh and Bazeley (1999) found that research proposal reviewers' evaluations of proposals were highly correlated with their evaluations of the researchers proposing the work. Furthermore, Jayasinghe et al. (2003) found that Australian Research Council proposals from more prestigious universities received higher ratings for the social sciences and humanities than for the hard sciences. They also showed that science proposals were rated higher when reviewers rated fewer proposals or were academics (i.e., professors vs. nonprofessors), suggesting a potential linkage between the reviewers, the type of work being proposed, and ratings.

It is important to remember, too, that gratuitously condescending, sarcastic, or ad hominem remarks can have a devastating effect, especially on young researchers, discouraging them from submitting further grant proposals (Hadjistavropoulos & Bieling, 2000). This may also result in the suppression of promising research careers. That such remarks can and do occur in reviews is well established (Epstein, 1995; Bedeian, 1996; Brysbaert, 1996; Fine, 1996; Levenson, 1996; Rabinovich, 1996), and an agency wishing to encourage proposals by new researchers may need to be especially sensitive to this.

Reviewer Ethics, Attitude, and Behavior

One of the authors recently had dinner with a professional colleague whom he had just met at a conference. In the course of table talk, the subject of reviewing journal articles came up. The colleague mentioned with great pride that a mutual friend and editor of a well-known journal always gave him the tough articles to review and that he always took authors of those articles to task. When asked what he meant by this comment, he proceeded to tell how he would utterly destroy the article with his questions and comments to the author. When asked if he thought that this might discourage the author from submitting other articles to the journal, he replied, again with pride, that he was almost sure it would. To us, this is the essence of one of the most serious ethical problems in the peer review process: the use of destructive comments and ad hominem remarks made to authors of articles and research proposals by peer reviewers, most often anonymously.

With the exception of The Society for Industrial and Organizational Psychologists (Lowman, 1998), which has made the review of articles for publication a major issue in its current code of ethics, professional psychological organizations have largely ignored the ethics of the peer review process. Hadjistavropoulos and Bieling (2000) have attempted to show how such gratuitous remarks and personal attacks by reviewers are a violation of the American Psychological Association's code of ethics. In examining the current APA code of ethics (American Psychological Association, 2002), one discovers that nothing directly addresses this issue of nasty, ad hominem reviews. Hadjistavropoulos and Bieling suggested that several sections of the APA code can and should be applied to reviewer behavior. They call particular attention to the wording in the APA ethics code (Principle A in the 2002 code change) that states: "Psychologists strive to benefit those with whom they work and take care to do no harm. In their professional actions, psychologists seek to safeguard the welfare and rights of those with whom they interact professionally. . . . " (p. 1062). One can also appeal to section 3.04, which calls for psychologists to do no harm to those with whom they work. The section (8.15) of the code that deals directly with reviewers only admonishes psychologists who review materials for presentation, publication, and grants to respect the confidentiality and proprietary rights of those submitting to review. It says nothing about the quality or tenor of those reviews. Clearly, the APA ethical code is weak and vague in addressing the issue of reviewer behaviors and is, in our opinion, in need of revision to correct this problem.

The Grants/Contracts Reviewing Process

Having established the basic principles of reviewing and their applicability to the grants/contract domain, we now turn to the actual review process. To provide more detailed guidance to grant and contract reviewers on how they might best complete their evaluations and fulfill their obligations to review proposals in an efficient, professional manner, we examine in some detail the proposal review process. Although the details of how different agencies carry out the process of making funding decisions about proposals can and do vary greatly, all use the following eight steps to some degree. First, the agencies typically spend a great deal of time and effort writing a formal statement of work on the proposed research topic. Second, an evaluation approach, including specific criteria for reviewing, grading systems, and weights, is developed. Third, the agency releases a formal Statement of Work (SOW) or Request for Proposals (RFP), which spells out the research requirements. Fourth, the agencies identify and solicit reviewers for the proposals. Fifth, the proposals are submitted and evaluated using the developed criteria. Sixth, the completed reviews are collapsed into a summary evaluation for each proposal. Seventh, decisions are made about which proposals to fund using the summary evaluations. Finally, winning proposals are funded, and authors of proposals not funded are debriefed and provided feedback on the decision.

We use this framework to discuss the review process and to illustrate what is expected of grant and contract proposal reviewers at each step in the process. Within this discussion, we raise issues that we think will be helpful to proposal reviewers and to the agencies that sponsor the research and employ the reviewers' services. This review process eventually links to the decision to award and fund a particular proposal and, as we have seen, the ramifications of providing effective and ethical reviews are substantial.

Describing the Work to Be Done

When reviewing for a funding agency, one of the first pieces of information an evaluator needs is the SOW/RFP. This document guided the authors who submitted proposals and should guide reviewers in their evaluations of them. Accordingly, it is worth briefly discussing the development of such documents and the impact they have on the review process.

The development of the SOW/RFP is perhaps the most important task in the grant/proposal process and one that, if done badly, makes the rest of the review process difficult, if not impossible. Proposal authors and reviewers alike are dependent on the written statements about what is to be done to guide their work. Thus, the SOW/RFP defines the rest of the review process. If the SOW/RFP is vague, unclear, conflicting, or insufficiently detailed, proposal authors will have an especially hard time responding. Authors can respond only to the information that is given to them about what a potential funding agency wants. If the agency does not write a clear and concise SOW/RFP, it will lead to ambiguous and general proposals. This in turn makes the job of the evaluators very difficult. It is unrealistic to expect that evaluators, who did not write the SOW/RFP, will be able to judge the extent to which a proposal will be able to meet the requirements of an SOW/RFP if those requirements are not spelled out in commonly understood language. That being the case, writing an SOW/RFP or proposal topic that clearly communicates the agency's requirements is the sine qua non of the proposal evaluation process.

Many agencies feel that if they knew how to do the research they wanted, they would not need to award a contract or grant. Supreme Court Justice Potter Stewart once said of pornography, "I shall not attempt further to define the kinds of material I understand to be embraced . . . but I know it when I see it" (*Jacobellis v. Ohio*, 1964). Similar notions in the research process often lead to vague descriptions of the research to be performed. As a result, reviewers spend most of their time individually or in meetings with agency personnel or other reviewers trying to figure out the intent of SOW/RFP. So, rather than expending energy determining which proposals have the best research approach, most of the reviewers' energy is expended in guessing what kind of research is wanted. Not only does this invariably result in lower quality proposals, it also assures a high probability that none of the proposals will trigger the "I know it when I see it" response.

There are two approaches to alleviating the problem of imprecise proposals. In the first approach, the agency relies on known and experienced researchers to do its work. Here, the agency and its SOW/RFP author already know what kind of research is wanted and have at least a generic idea of how to do this research. In this approach the SOW/RFP author is trusted by the organization to produce an SOW/RFP that clearly communicates the research intent. Unfortunately, although this leads to clearer proposals, this approach tends to create an insular group of "trusted" researchers and limits the variety of proposals funded and topics investigated. In the second approach, all SOW/RFPs must pass through a review mechanism. In this mechanism the SOW/RFP is read for clarity of desired results and possibility of research accomplishment. Those SOW/RFPs that are not adequate are returned to authors with suggestions for improvement. The latter approach will produce more reliably high-quality proposals, but at the expense of more time expended and some potential for negative effects on the morale of potential researchers.

For reviewers of the SOW/RFP itself, there are two key points to remember: First, the SOW/RFP is an important marker of agency needs and interests. Agency research agendas evolve over time, and the SOW/RFP represents not only the funding agency's research priorities but also reveals something about the history of the organization and its past projects, successes, and failures. For example, one military agency has a long history of investing in research about leadership and its development among that service's officers. Leadership and leader development studies in several areas were supported, but the ones that showed the most promise, in this case studies of leader intelligence and problem solving, led to a particular emphasis on these topics in several subsequent RFPs.

The second key point to remember is that the SOW/RFP explicitly or implicitly tells proposers what the evaluation criteria are. Thus, if the research agenda is highly technical, then areas of emphasis in evaluation are also likely to be technical in nature. The way the SOW/RFP is written can point to other nontechnical criteria such as a focus on new researchers, interdisciplinary efforts, or research employing social scientific methods.

Accordingly, it is very important for proposal reviewers to become familiar with the SOW/RFP and the funding agency's stated areas of research interest.

Evaluation Approaches

As a proposal reviewer, it is important to understand the evaluation approach being used by the funding agency and the reasons for it. Being aware of the approach can help guide the reviewer by demonstrating what factors are of particular importance to the agency, which ones are less so, and what factors are to be ignored completely.

There are typically two formal approaches to proposal evaluations: overall impression and bottom-up. With the overall impression approach, reviewers are asked to make an omnibus evaluation of the proposal and then justify that rating with specific examples, dimension evaluations, and criticisms. In this way, the overall approach is not that different from many journal review processes in which the evaluator often is asked to make an "Accept" or "Reject" recommendation and then support that recommendation with specific comments and criticisms.

The overall approach is often easier for the reviewer as he or she can read the entire proposal, formulate an impression based on his or her unspecified criteria, and then look for specifics to support that impression. Unfortunately for the agency, this approach is less useful as it is clearly prone to common rater errors such as halo (negative or positive) and leniency and severity biases. Some rather large funding agencies, the NSF for example, use the overall approach. The NSF sets two broad criteria for evaluators to use: "What is the intellectual merit of the proposed activity?" and, "What are the broader impacts of the proposed activities?" Within this broad framework, the NSF provides suggestions for the reviewer to consider for each of the criteria. However, reviewers are to provide an overall rating for each proposal and a summary statement that includes comments on both of these general criteria.

The second, and perhaps more common, approach is bottom-up, usually with multiple and specific dimensions. In this approach, reviewers are provided with a list of specific dimensions that are to be rated and then, after making individual dimension ratings, reviewers are asked to provide an overall assessment of the proposal based on the dimension ratings. Bottom-up ratings place greater demands of time and effort on reviewers because they must read and rate every proposal on all of the listed dimensions. Conversely, agencies like this approach because it affords better comparability across proposals, which is key for making funding decisions and works to minimize common rater bias errors. This approach is often the evaluation approach used by Department of Defense agencies.

If the bottom-up approach is used, the agency will have to develop the dimensions and their weights. The major challenge here is to select meaningful and important dimensions that are relatively independent from one another. That is, the evaluation needs to be based on a set of independent (to minimize halo) and differentially weighted (to maximize prediction) dimensions. Across a broad range of agencies we informally surveyed, we found that most bottom-up evaluation approaches contain some version of the following dimensions:

1. *Importance of research goal from the funding organization's point of view.* This generally is operationalized by the extent to which the proposal fits into one or more of the research areas described in the SOW/RFP. This goal should follow directly from the SOW/RFP and the extent to which the proposed research meets the funding agency's objectives.
2. *Quality of technical approach.* This is generally operationalized as the appropriateness of the methods, subjects, and measures as well as the sophistication and thoroughness of the research design.
3. *Quality of researchers.* This is generally operationalized as the experience, qualifications, and expertise of the primary investigator and, secondarily, of the research team.

As we have seen, the third dimension is also the factor that can have a strong halo effect on the other evaluation factors. Famous and experienced individuals may be assumed to be expert researchers, and such inferences often bleed over into the ratings for technical approach and importance. By making researcher quality an explicit evaluation factor, agencies hope to curb these halo effects.

Of these three, the technical approach is often the most difficult to judge. There are many ways to accomplish a particular research objective, and an extensive knowledge of methods and design is often necessary to rate not only a particular proposal but also to make comparisons on methods across proposals written by individuals from a wide variety of disciplines. Thus, for the proposal reviewer, becoming familiar with a variety of methodological approaches and also with the preferred or typical methods used by funded researchers is an important prerequisite for evaluating the technical approach section. A cautionary note here, however, is that reviewers and funding agencies should keep in mind that creative and innovative approaches may be excluded erroneously simply because they imaginatively propose different and unusual approaches that are not in the current zeitgeist.

The bottom-up approach may include other dimensions. Our survey identified dimensions such as relevance to the organization (different from importance), likelihood of transition from research to practice, affordability (although external reviewers are often not in a position to judge this, internal evaluators often are), and the proposing organization's support and infrastructure.

Turning to the independence of dimensions, as noted, the quality of researchers frequently seems to carry over into the goodness of the technical approach and other dimensions. To minimize this halo effect, this dimension is often put last or near the end of the evaluation process. Furthermore, this effect can be ameliorated by a blind review in which evaluators judge the technical approach without knowing who the researchers are. The added administrative complications may mitigate against such an approach, however. For the reviewer, keeping in mind the intended independence of the dimensions and the need to minimize halo bias, especially when reviewing the proposals of prominent researchers, is important for ensuring consistent and accurate reviews.

There are a variety of scoring systems that are used to provide ratings. Typically, these systems are numerical, allowing for easy combination of dimension scores into an overall evaluation and facilitating comparison among proposals. Scoring approaches are often manipulated so that the highest combined score for a given proposal is 100, thereby making it similar to classroom scoring and providing the evaluator with a basis for comparison. The scoring approach may incorporate differential weights, and such weighting systems may or may not be visible to the reviewer. For example, one agency weights technical merit and relevance to the organization at 25 points each, whereas investigator qualifications and institutional facilities are worth only 5 points each. The issue for the reviewer to keep in mind is that if differential weights are employed, the specific weights assigned to dimensions send a signal, intentional or not, to the reviewer about the relative importance of the various dimensions.

The issue of scoring and weighting of factors is a difficult one. Some agencies have argued that there would be greater utility in using a multiple hurdle strategy, whereby each proposal has to be rated at a certain level on one or more gatekeeper dimensions before being considered further. For example, one agency uses an "Importance of the Research to This Organization" dimension in such a way. If the proposal is rated "Not Important," then the rating process stops and the proposal is rejected. Other funding agencies have implemented a blind weighting system whereby there are underlying weights associated with each dimension but the reviewers are not privy to those weights. This may serve to minimize rater inconsistency but adds to the complexity and length of the evaluation process, delaying the final funding decisions. There is also movement in some agencies to replace numerical scores with other rating schemes, colors, words, letter grades, graphics, and so forth. Unfortunately, at some point the various dimension scores will need to be collapsed to produce an overall score per evaluation, and the scores of the individual evaluators will have to be collapsed to produce a summary score per proposal. Non-numerical scores cannot be summarized without the intervention of the agency and its personnel, adding additional layers of effort and complexity to the process. Further, if the program director or evaluation chief is put in the position of having to use non-numerical scoring, that chief will need to provide the evaluators with an informal mechanism for converting the non-numerical scores into numbers and then back into the non-numerical format. Whatever the mechanism used, it needs to be consistently applied across evaluators. One approach to ensure consistency across reviewers might be to use letter grades (A, B, C, D, and F) and informally assign numbers to the letters (A = 4, B = 3, etc.) in a traditional grade point average format. Regardless of the evaluation approach used, the system in place provides useful information to the reviewer. Combined with the information in the SOW/RFP, the dimensions and weighting systems used provide critical context about the funding agency's objectives and values.

Announcing the Research Requirement

For the reviewer, the actual announcement procedure is of less importance than what the announcement says. As noted previously, the SOW/RFP helps the reviewer to understand what types and areas of research the agency has funded in the past and intends to fund in the future. To that extent, reviewers should examine the funding announcement for several important pieces of information.

First, the announcement will include a description of the funding organization designed to provide potential proposal authors and reviewers with a reasonable idea of the audience for the proposal. Funding organizations might include military branches, scientific agencies, governmental entities (departments, state and local governments, etc.), or nonprofits (foundations, charities, nongovernmental aid organizations, etc.). Recognizing the audience for the proposals can help the reviewer to understand organizational objectives and priorities. Next, the announcement should include a description of the research requested at a meaningful level (i.e., the SOW/RFP). As noted previously, the SOW/RFP spells out the funding agency's research priorities, its history, and past projects as well as revealing information about evaluation criteria, areas of emphasis, and other relevant information.

Beyond the organizational and SOW/RFP information, the announcement will also include instructions on how to apply for funding, instructions for submitting proposals, and other administrative guidance such as formatting and submission deadlines. Here, there might be information on exactly what sections should be in the technical and cost proposals, where and when to apply, and other application criteria. Finally, the announcement may include information about which sections of the proposal are the most important in terms of the evaluation. For example, if the funding agency is using the multiple hurdle approach, then importance of research is likely to be emphasized in the announcement. Other examples of announcements emphasizing particular aspects of the proposals include one agency that lists "Technical Approach" and "Organizational Relevance" first and weights them most heavily.

Although the SOW/RFP is the most important part of the announcement with which the reviewers should become familiar, other aspects, including organizational history and context, audience, and evaluation criteria, provide useful guidance to reviewers in helping them to formulate their evaluations.

Identifying Evaluators

The identification and selection of evaluators will be done by the granting agency, usually without any input from the evaluators themselves. However, some agencies, such as the NSF, will accept unsolicited offers from scientists who wish to review proposals. This is something that all psychologists should consider. Being a reviewer for publications and grants is a professional duty that we should all be willing to share. Furthermore, this is a very good way for young professionals to learn about the grant/contracting process and to become known to one's more senior and influential colleagues. That said, as a reviewer it is important to know who the other reviewers are, including their affiliations, orientations, and disciplines. If, for example, most of the reviewers are internal to the organization, they will typically focus on organization-specific issues such as fit, funding, and previous research. This allows external reviewers to focus on issues such as the quality and impact of the research on the

broader scientific community or its potential to lead to presentation and publication. Similarly, if, for a given proposal, most of
the reviewers are experimental psychologists, it may be important for the remaining reviewer or reviewers to focus on aspects
of the research that they are uniquely capable of assessing, such
as the qualitative aspects of the research or relevant sociological
theories. Beyond these areas, the characteristics and rating tendencies of other evaluators, though of critical importance to the
funding agency, are typically not of substantive importance to
any particular reviewer.

Evaluating Proposals

Once the reviewer is comfortable with the organization's objectives, the SOW/RFP, and the research agenda, he or she is ready
to begin the review process. One issue the reviewer should be-
ware of before starting to read and rate is whether the proposals
are to be evaluated in terms of the formal scale (criterion referenced) or whether they are to be compared with each other (norm
referenced). The usual approach is criterion referenced, but if there
are many proposals on the same topic, a relative comparison approach might be of greater use to the funding agency.

Reviewers also need to be aware of de jure and de facto guidelines and criteria that will be in play during the evaluation process. De jure, or formal, criteria consist of the evaluation forms,
written guidance, scales, grading systems, and so forth. These
criteria are what the agency says it wants used. However, there
are almost always de facto, or informal, criteria that also guide
the process. In some organizations, these informal policies and
procedures affecting the rating process may be even more important than official, stated policies.

These informal policies typically fall into one of two categories.
The first has to do with what aspects of the proposals to be rated
are really most important. Although the formal rating scale may
weight technical approach highest, in many organizations the fit
between the focus of the research and the funding organization's
broader objectives—be they scientific, political, or personal—is
inevitably the important factor. That is, if the research does not
help advance the organization's objectives, it probably will not

get funded no matter how technically solid it is. Although some funding agencies formalize this policy via the two-tiered rating systems mentioned previously, others do not make such official distinctions. As a rater, it is important to determine what the informal criteria are and how they differ from the formal policies spelled out in the instructions and training.

The second type of informal policy deals with which proposals actually get funded. The typical formal funding policy may prescribe that the scores of each proposal are summarized, all of the proposals are ranked by score, and then the proposals are funded from number one down until the money runs out. However, the connection between final score and funding decision may be less direct. As already noted, there may be organizational, political, or personal factors that affect the funding decision beyond simple ratings. Thus, reviewers of multiple proposals may not necessarily be able to increase the chances of funding by scoring a proposal very high or to lessen the chances of funding by scoring it very low. The implication for proposal reviewers is that they need to be aware, or to try and learn about, such informal policies before commencing their reviewing process.

How might a reviewer gain such information? There are several sources for such information. First, a thorough reading of current and past SOW/RFPs and previously funded proposals, if possible, is helpful. By comparing funded proposals with calls for research, the reviewer can begin to identify informal policies and their impact on the review process and funding decisions. Second, the reviewer can initiate discussions with funding agency personnel. Program managers, contracting officers, and agency research personnel are all good sources of information about informal polices and practices.

The effect that such information has on the reviewer is variable. Some reviewers may opt not to participate in a process where the criteria are informal and undocumented. Other reviewers might see such information as useful guides for their own reviews. Regardless of the response, being aware of the variety of formal and informal criteria, their interplay, and the effect that they have on the review process is important contextual information for the new reviewer.

Collapsing Individual Evaluations

Because multiple raters will read most proposals, these scores need to be collapsed into a single indicator. Some of the smaller agencies reported using 2 to 5 raters per proposal, but some of the larger ones reported that up to 200 individuals read some submissions, because each reviewer may only read a few sections of each proposal if they are especially long or complicated. There are several ways that the scores may be combined. First, agencies may use a consensus discussion method. Here, the reviewers read and rate each proposal independently and then get together to discuss their thoughts. A discussion ensues, and a final rating is agreed on by the entire group. These discussions may occur face to face or by telephone. This approach is rather time consuming but often leads to a better understanding of the proposal and agreement as to its merits, limitations, and viability. Furthermore, the funding agency can guide the discussion and focus it to ensure that a consensus is reached. Again, a word of caution is in order. It is important to remember that research has shown that such discussions tend to reinforce individual reviewers' opinions, especially when they follow the majority or at least the most strongly voiced opinions. Program managers and evaluation chiefs need to keep this in mind as they strive for consensus.

An alternative approach is mechanical combination or averaging. With this technique, the rater's scores are simply averaged to generate a final score. A third approach is a qualitative version of the second whereby funding agency personnel, either the proposal coordinator or the program head, qualitatively combine individual ratings into a holistic evaluation of each proposal. This technique is more common if there are also informal policies guiding the review process, especially if criteria such as organizational fit, political considerations, or personal preference affect the funding decision.

Debriefing Authors of Nonfunded Proposals

Once funding decisions have been made, most agencies provide feedback to the authors of the winning proposals and those that were not funded. This is a very important step in the process as it helps shape current research and provides feedback to authors who may be resubmitting in the future. For authors of proposals that were not funded, feedback on why the proposal was not chosen, what could be improved, or, if appropriate, the opinion that the research stream may never be funded, will help authors with future submissions. Sternberg (2004) advised those submitting grant applications that first proposals are often rejected, but paying attention to such feedback, revising, and resubmitting the proposal can often result in success in a subsequent funding round. For contract winners, such feedback can provide information on changes, additions, and deletions to the research that will improve its chances of success, its fit in the organization, and its likelihood of contributing to broader organizational objectives.

The feedback process is also useful to reviewers. Having the funding agency provide information to reviewers on which proposals were funded and why, how other reviewers rated the same proposals, and constructive criticism on their own reviews helps individuals to be better reviewers the next time. The funding agency itself also benefits from a thorough review and feedback process, the results of which can lead to modifying future SOW/RFPs, the reviewer selection process, the evaluation process, and funding decisions.

The actual debriefing process varies across agencies. It is clear that the process should be carried out in the most informative and helpful way possible because the information provided might lead to later successful proposals. This suggests that the feedback process provide as much detail as possible about why a given proposal was unsuccessful. For pure feedback purposes, written debriefings that can be carefully crafted, using excerpts or quotations from the original reviews, and that spell out in a detailed letter why the proposal was not funded are best. Keep in mind that some agencies submit all reviewer comments verbatim to their respective proposal writers as part of the review process. Such letters can be kept, re-read by the proposal author, and used when revising the proposals. Unfortunately, the litigiousness of today's society has forced some agencies to provide little or no feedback for fear that anything that is said can and will be used against the agency in a lawsuit by a nonfunded author. In this case, written feedback letters can be kept and used as the basis of legal suits.

An alternative feedback approach is to provide verbal debriefings in person. Such interactive sessions might result in closer collaboration and more useful, often informal, information passing between the agency and the author. However, such face-to-face personal interactions can sometimes degenerate to hostilities that can be very difficult to terminate. Another approach is to provide telephone debriefings. These allow for interaction and information exchange, but produce no written record, providing legal cover, and can be easily terminated if things start to go bad. Several agency chiefs suggested that telephone debriefings seem to have the fewest disadvantages.

Final Comments

As a summary of the information about the peer review process presented in this chapter, we suggest reviewers consider taking the following steps:

Become a Reviewer

If you are asked to be a reviewer in your area of expertise, accept. If you are not asked, volunteer. Agencies are always in need of competent reviewers. Not only is it a professional duty to be part of the peer review process, but also you will grow professionally as a result of the experience. This is especially true, we think, in becoming a reviewer of grant/contract proposals. Here you will get a firsthand look at the process and what makes a fundable proposal. This will help you in developing good proposals of your own.

Read the SOW/RFP

Once you have been selected to be a reviewer, be sure to read the SOW/RFP for the proposals you are to evaluate. Look for clues about what the agency's research needs are. Remember that you are looking for explicit and implicit requirements. You also want to get a sense of the history of the agency's research requirements. Three major questions to ask yourself as you read the SOW/RFP are as follows: What is the importance of this research to the agency and what role will that likely play in the evaluation process? How will technical quality be defined and how important is that in determining the evaluation outcome? How will the quality of the research personnel be evaluated, explicitly or implicitly, and how will this be used in the evaluation process?

Read the Announcement

To get further insight into the review process and what the agency wants, be sure to read the announcement that the agency puts out to solicit proposals. Use the same criteria that you used in reading the SOW/RFP to get more information about what the agency has told submitters that it wants.

Other Reviewers

Find out, if you can, who the other reviewers will be. This will give you some insight on how you may use your expertise in the review process. It may also tell you how the agency sees your role in the review process.

The Evaluation Process

Learn about the evaluation process, formal and informal. This means combining the review guidelines you are given by the agency with what you already know from reading the announcement and the SOW/RFP, knowing who the other reviewers are, and gathering information from agency personnel. Do not be afraid to ask questions of the agency personnel who are managing the review process. As you get a better idea of the review process, be sure to look for how biases may enter into the process and formulate ways to avoid them.

Feedback to Submitters

Make sure you understand how your recommendations, remarks, and comments will be used in the review process. You especially need to know whether your review results will be combined with others in providing feedback and whether your comments will be given verbatim to the proposal authors. Ideally, you will be able to review the feedback given to authors before the agency sends it out.

Feedback to Reviewers

Many agencies will provide feedback to reviewers. If it is not routinely provided by the agency conducting the review, then ask for it. Being a reviewer is a learning experience as well as a professional duty.

Finally, above all else, be professional. Being a reviewer is an opportunity for you to grow, to help your colleagues to grow, and to advance the science of psychology. Use it wisely and ethically.

References

American Psychological Association. (2002). Ethical principles of psychologists and code of conduct. *American Psychologist, 57,* 1060–1073.

Bedeian, A. G. (1996). Improving the journal review process: The question of ghostwriting. *American Psychologist, 51,* 1189.

Boice, R., Pecker, G., Zaback, E., & Barlow D. H. (1985). A challenge to Peters and Cici's conclusions with an examination of editorial files for reviewer appropriateness. *Behavioral and Brain Sciences, 8,* 744–745.

Brysbaert, M. (1996). Improving the journal review process and the risk of making the poor poorer. *American Psychologist, 51,* 1193.

Coley, S. M., & Scheinberg, C. A. (2000). *Proposal writing* (2nd ed.). Thousand Oaks, CA: Sage.

Drotar, D. (2000). Reviewing and editing manuscripts for scientific journals. In D. Drotar (Ed.), *Handbook of research in pediatric and clinical psychology* (pp. 409–424). New York: Kluwer Academic/Plenum.

Epstein, S. (1995). What can be done to improve the journal review process. *American Psychologist, 50,* 883–885.

Fine, M. A. (1996). Reflections on enhancing accountability in the peer review process, not the review process. *American Psychologist, 51,* 1190–1191.

Hadjistavropoulos, T., & Bieling, P. J. (2000). When reviews attack: Ethics, free speech, and the peer review process. *Canadian Psychology, 41,* 152–159.

Hemlin, S. (1999). (Dis)Agreement in peer review. In P. Juslin & H. Montgomery (Eds.), *Judgment and decision making: Neo-Brunswickian and process-tracing approaches* (pp. 275–301). Mahwah, NJ: Erlbaum.

Jacobellis v. Ohio, 378 U.S. 184, 197 (1964).

Jayasinghe, U. W., Marsh, H. W., & Bond, N. (2003). A multilevel cross-classified modeling approach to peer review of grant proposals: The effects of assessor and researcher attributes on assessor ratings. *Journal of the Royal Statistical Society Series A—Statistics in Society, 166,* 279–300.

Levenson, R. L., Jr. (1996). Enhancing the journals, not the review process. *American Psychologist, 51,* 1191–1193.

Lowman, R. L. (1998). *The ethical practice of psychology in organizations.* Washington, DC: American Psychological Association.

Marsh, H. W., & Bazeley, P. (1999). Multiple evaluations of grant proposals by independent assessors: Confirmatory factor analysis evaluations of reliability, validity, and structure. *Multivariate Behavioral Research, 34,* 1–30.

Norman, K. L. (1986). Importance of factors in the review of grant proposals. *Journal of Applied Psychology, 71,* 156–162.

Rabinovich, B. A. (1996). A perspective on the journal peer review process, not the review process. *American Psychologist, 51,* 1190.

Stamper, H. (1995). The review process. In W. Pequegnat & E. Stover (Eds.), *How to write a successful research grant application: A guide for social scientists* (pp. 47–54). New York: Plenum Press.

Sternberg, R. J. (2004). Obtaining a research grant: The applicant's view. In J. M. Darley, M. P. Zanna, & H. L. Roediger III (Eds.), *The complete academic: A career guide* (2nd ed., pp. 169–184). Washington, DC: American Psychological Association.

Index

About the Editor

Robert J. Sternberg, PhD, is best known for his theory of success-ful intelligence, investment theory of creativity (developed with Todd Lubart), theory of mental self-government, balance theory of wisdom, triangular theory of love, and theory of love as a story. Dr. Sternberg is the author of more than 900 journal articles, book chapters, and books and has received about $20 million in government grants and contracts for his research. He was president of the American Psychological Association (APA) in 2003 and currently is editor of *Contemporary Psychology*. He received his PhD from Stanford University in 1975 and his BA summa cum laude, Phi Beta Kappa, from Yale University in 1972. He has won many awards from APA and other organizations. He has been president of four APA divisions and has served as editor of *Psychological Bulletin*.